## PRAISE FOR *FIND A QUIET CORNER*

"O'Hara helps us find the quiet place inside us where inner peace abounds. In our harried lives, it's comforting to remember the quiet place can be revisited."

—Michele Weiner-Davis, M.S.W., author of
*Fire Your Shrink* and *Divorce Busting*

"*Find a Quiet Corner* is a wise and inspirational book, a beautiful introduction to the art of meditation. The book offers a helping hand along the path toward inner peace and happiness. We will all ultimately walk this path. Why not begin now?"

—Brian L. Weiss, M.D., P.A., author of
*Many Lives, Many Masters*

"To pause, to breathe, to sense, to be—these gaps in the busy-ness are what give meaning to activity. *Find a Quiet Corner* is a precious guide and reminder to live from the spaciousness of our inner beings—to live in the joy and peace that are our birthright."

—Joan Borysenko, Ph.D., author of
*Guilt Is the Teacher, Love Is the Lesson*

"There is a breathtaking wisdom and strength to be found in a single moment of silence—and Nancy O'Hara offers a kind invitation to listen. *Find a Quiet Corner* is a gentle opening; it beckons us into a fruitful practice. Here, we harvest the compelling grace that is born only in the quiet of our lives."

—Wayne Muller, author of *Sabbath: Finding
Rest, Renewal, and Delight in Our Busy Lives*

## PRAISE FOR *JUST LISTEN*

"Men and women alike will find much wisdom and quiet strength in these pages. *Just Listen* is an eloq
we all desire."

—John Gray, aut
*Women Are from*

"This is a clear, beautiful book that can help everyone. O'Hara's writing is fine, compassionate, and always has a ring of truth. To learn to listen is to turn the world around."

—Natalie Goldberg, author of *Writing Down the Bones* and *Long Quiet Highway*

"This book is a searchlight illuminating the wisdom and power of inner life. It will help anyone discover serenity and peace, which we need in our hectic times more than ever before."

—Larry Dossey, M.D., author of *Be Careful What You Pray For, Prayer Is Good Medicine,* and *Healing Words*

"O'Hara's practical guide to just listening places a gentle woman's hand on the daily practice of meditation."

—Perle Besserman, author of *Owning It: Zen and the Art of Facing Life*

"Breathe deeply, relax your body, empty your mind, and read Nancy O'Hara's *Just Listen.* She gently guides you on the path to experiencing greater serenity and discovering the passionate life you were born to live."

—Robert Gerzon, author of *Finding Serenity in the Age of Anxiety*

"This is a simple book in the best sense of the word. It is a profound book and, because it comes from Nancy O'Hara's firsthand experience, it penetrates the heart, guiding the reader in the right direction."

—Eido T. Shimano, Abbot, Dai Bosatsu Zendo

# NANCY O'HARA

THREE RIVERS PRESS
NEW YORK

*Seven*

*Steps*

*to*

# WORK

# ■ FROM THE ■

# INSIDE OUT

*Loving*

*What*

*You*

*Do*

Published by Three Rivers Press, New York, New York.
Member of the Crown Publishing Group.

Random House, Inc. New York, Toronto, London, Sydney, Auckland
www.randomhouse.com

THREE RIVERS PRESS is a registered trademark and the Three Rivers Press colophon is a trademark of Random House, Inc.

Printed in the United States of America

Design by Jennifer Ann Daddio

Library of Congress Cataloging-in-Publication Data
O'Hara, Nancy.
Work from the inside out: seven steps to loving what you do /
by Nancy O'Hara.
1. Job satisfaction.    2. Quality of work life.    3. Spiritual life.
4. Satisfaction.    I. Title.

HF5549.5.J63 O39    2001
650.1—dc21
00-066676

ISBN 0-609-80592-4

1   3   5   7   9   10   8   6   4   2

First Edition

*To all my students and readers,*
*who give me the opportunity to do what*
*I love doing, however flawed it may be.*

# ACKNOWLEDGMENTS

∎

I owe an enormous debt of gratitude to many people, beginning with Eido Shimano Roshi, my teacher; Sarah Jane Freymann, my agent and friend; and Boun Nancy Berg, my spiritual guide.

While all of the names and some of the details of the personal stories in this book have been changed to protect privacy, some of those who have graciously shared their work stories with me have chosen to remain nameless even here. With palms together I bow deeply to you all. Scott Burrows, Barbara Lee, Patty Michaud-Moerlins, Nanette Miller, Colleen O'Hara, Karen O'Hara, Michael O'Hara, and Barbara Suter—thank you for your open and willing spirits.

To all my Dharma sisters and brothers who continue to inspire me with their ceaseless energy and commitment to work practice, I humbly send my heartfelt thanks and appreciation. And a special thanks to everyone I have worked for and with over the years. I have learned most of this from all of you.

I am also indebted to Walpola Rahula's book, *What the Buddha Taught.* It is the one I keep going back to. With its simplicity and thoroughness, it continues to instruct and inspire me.

And, finally, thanks to all those at Three Rivers Press (including those unnamed and at this moment unknown to me) in whose good and capable hands this book now rests: Chip Gibson, Becky Cabaza and Carrie Thornton, to name but a few. And thank you, Patricia Gift, for your early enthusiasm and support. Good luck in your new venture.

If I have forgotten anyone, please forgive me. It is not due to lack of gratitude but simply lack of perfection. And Ann Levy, here you are at last. Thank you.

# CONTENTS

■

# WORK
# · FROM THE ·
# INSIDE OUT

# INTRODUCTION

■

I love to rake leaves. I don't get to do it often (which might account for why I love it) since I live in a city and have no backyard. But when I visit my mother in the fall in New England, where leaves are plentiful, I am the first to volunteer for the job of clearing them away. There are a number of reasons why I love raking leaves. One, I don't have to think too hard; I know what I have to do and how to do it. Two, it engages my entire being—my body (the physical act of raking), my mind (the little decisions that must be made of where to start, how big the piles should be, when to bag the leaves) and my spirit (being in the midst of nature awakens in me a sense of wonder and awe)—so that I become fully involved on every level with the task before me. Three, it is immediately rewarding—the leaves accumulate into piles and then into bags before my very eyes just by my moving the rake over and over and over again. Even though I appreciate the leaf-free lawn and can see the results of my work, I often just want to keep on raking. It's a happy result, but the point of the job is not the leaf-free lawn. The point of the job is simply raking, raking, raking. Four, I get to spend time outdoors engaged in an activity when I might otherwise be sitting inside. This allows me to fully appreciate the autumn and the changing of the seasons. And I always experience deep gratitude for my physical ability to rake, for my good fortune in having a mother who has a backyard that needs raking, for my mother, for my life. I don't even mind if my siblings who also might be visiting don't pitch in to help. I realize that not everyone feels the same way about it that I do, and besides, the more rakers, the less work for me. I'm happy just to have them there to visit with. And it's a meditative exercise for me. I can practice being fully in each moment as I concentrate on simply raking. It's an opportunity for me to hone my awareness and develop mindfulness.

I could go on about the pleasures I derive from raking leaves, but I think you probably get the point. And it is this spirit, this state of mind, that we can all learn to bring to any task, and most especially to our daily work so that we can live each day fully and richly, content and satisfied at the day's end, knowing that we've given our all. And if we bring to the everyday the reverence we normally reserve for the sacred, then our spiritual life will inform our work life and our whole life will be a seamless web of grace.

So whatever tasks we are engaged in each day, whether it's raking leaves, running a company or selling stocks and bonds, if we bring a mindful attitude with us, we can accomplish whatever we put our minds to *and* be spiritually fulfilled. There's nothing quite like the feeling one gets from a job well done, or the feeling at the end of a long and difficult project or day of work when you know you've done your best. Contented peace of mind? Joyful fatigue? Overall wellness? However you describe such a sensation, chances are you've experienced it, even if its origin wasn't work. You need only look at your play activities or hobbies and the good feelings they generate to understand this sensibility. Even if you've never experienced such feelings in relationship to work and can only connect them to traditional "fun" activities, I promise that if you take the suggestions outlined in this book, at some point work will again, or perhaps for the first time, become fun and a source of rich and deep feelings of satisfaction. And your spirit—your inner essence, your true nature—will become fully awakened.

Most of us have to work these days. And many of us view our work as simply a means to an end—a way to generate income to pay for what we need to live our lives and give us the things that make us happy. Maybe we envisioned work providing meaning to our lives, but somewhere along the way those ideals were crushed and our expectations went unmet. Yet the very fact that we had, or may even still have, expectations about our work is the reason we continue to experience disappointment. Becoming aware of and acknowledging those dashed expectations can be the perfect starting place to adopt a new outlook on work, or to return to our youthful attitude toward work as something that can endow our life with meaning. In fact, disappointment stemming from expectation might even be the impetus we need to be open to change and to look closely at how we approach work. In *Work from the Inside Out: Seven Steps to Loving What You Do* we'll explore expectations (and yours in particular) in detail. We'll look at how anticipation can turn into expectation, disappointment, anger and pain. And we'll learn how to identify and eliminate expectations in our life and return to the simpler and purer impulse of anticipation, which will open us up to the unexpected and bring joy to our hearts.

It is in the arena of work, and particularly in our day-to-day work lives, that many of us experience the sharpest, deepest and perhaps most bitter disappointments. We expected work to give back to us everything we put into it and more. We expected work to satisfy our inner yearning for meaning. We expected those around us to do their jobs as well as we do ours. We expected our company to take care of us. Occasionally we even expected something just for showing up each day. Or we expected that we would eventually work in a job we loved and that our current work would be temporary; we didn't expect it to last so long, to become our vocation. We expected one thing; we received something else; we experienced disappointment. As a result, we lost whatever meaning there once was in work, and we even *expect* to be disappointed with our work.

*This can all change.* We *can* find meaning in work. But first we have to do a little work on ourselves and shift our perspective away from our old expectations. We must change the way we approach our jobs. We must foster a willingness to enjoy each and every task put before us and put aside all expectations of what the completion of any one particular chore might bring. In exchange we must settle for the reward that lies in the very doing of each and every task. While this may sound easy, it's not. Simple, yes. Easy, no. But it's worth taking the risk to unlearn everything you've worked so hard to know about work, and start over. It's worth it because if you do, you will experience a freedom in your work life that you've never known before. You will achieve a level of happiness with yourself that will permeate all areas of your life. The fear of losing what you have and not getting what you want will recede until it is only a dim memory. You will intuitively know what choices to make and which situations to avoid. And you will find yourself in a job you love, doing what you love doing, and loving what you do.

But first there's some work to be done. And if you can begin by adopting an attitude of "I love doing this" rather than "I can't wait to get this over with," it will all be easier and the rewards will manifest immediately.

So as you work through the exercises in *Work from the Inside Out,* keep your heart and mind focused on the following suggestions. And remember, this is about you;

this is your life. You will find your own answers. They will not look like anyone else's. No grades will be given. You are on your own. Your life—and this includes your work life—is entirely in your hands and up to you. And if you are gentle with and understanding of yourself as you move through change toward the unexpected, your journey will be filled with joy.

> *The whole world says that my teaching is great but*
> *unconventional. This unconventionality is precisely why it*
> *is great. If it were conventional it would already be*
> *small and insignificant. I have three treasures for you to*
> *cherish.*
> *The first is compassion.*
> *The second is simplicity.*
> *The third is patience.*
> *With compassion you will find courage.*
> *With simplicity you will know how to be generous.*
> *With patience you will surely move ahead.*
> *If you attempt to force things and do without the*
> *three treasures, you will surely die.*
> *If you practice the three treasures you will be blessed with a*
> *compassionate life.*
>
> TAO TE CHING (#67)

*Keep it simple.* Don't allow frustration with the process to control you. When you notice yourself projecting into the future and wondering how any of this will improve your work life, trust that all will be revealed in time. Bring yourself back to the present moment. Don't complicate that which is inherently simple.

*Be patient.* Certain exercises in this book will ask you to do some internal housecleaning, others will ask you to pay attention to your behavior over a period of time and some will ask you to do nothing. Don't rush things. If you trust in the process and put your heart into it, the rewards will begin immediately. They may not look the way you expected them to, but they will be there and they will multiply as you move along. And while you're at it, don't forget to breathe.

*Be compassionate toward yourself.* The truth of your work life and how you approach it will be revealed to you if you do the work that is suggested here. In the process you might get in touch with the tender and vulnerable side of yourself. Feelings will be exposed. Bad habits will be revealed. Some discomfort will set in. This is natural. Give yourself a break. Allow yourself the space to feel new things (and some old things) as you grow. Throughout the book there will be tools for coping. And remember that the compassion you nurture for yourself will spill forth into the world and reach others. You will be available to yourself and others in a way that you never have been before.

*Simplicity, patience, compassion.* Keep these in the forefront of your mind and look inside your heart as you move toward work that fulfills and nourishes you. Write these three words down: *simplicity, patience, compassion.* Say them out loud each morning when you awake to remind yourself of your mission. Include them in your prayers. Use them as mantras throughout the day. Each day as you are faced with situations, problems, confusions, decisions, confrontations, pleasures, take a deep breath before responding (or worse, reacting) and bring your mind to these three themes—simplicity, patience, compassion. See if you can draw on one or all of them for inspiration, courage, strength and whatever else you need. Let these words be your spiritual escorts. They will always be there when you call on them. They will not fail you.

It is human nature to want to know the end of the story (or how this book will help you), so here's a preview of what you can expect from each section and the progression that will take you to the blessed state of loving what you do and doing what you love.

Chapter 1, "Understanding and Acceptance," will help you to define exactly what it is about your work life that is so disagreeable to you. It will also reveal to you what your role in your own discomfort has been. As painful as it might be to examine this relationship, it will be necessary so that you can come to an understanding of what your problems with work are and move beyond them.

Once you clearly understand where your dissatisfaction lies, you can then investigate the causes. In Chapter 2, "Seeing Clearly and Letting Go," we will look at cause and effect, the reasons for your unhappiness, the how and why of it all. Here is where you will begin the process of letting go. We will also "follow the money"— its meaning in your life, your attitudes toward it, how it works and doesn't work for you, where it fits in the whole scheme of things, and how you can have money and still lead a spiritual life.

In Chapter 3, "Realizing This Is It!" you'll learn that you can and must change in order to move forward and find satisfaction in your work. You will see that the key to change is action. And you'll learn how acceptance of what is and freedom from what isn't can lead you to a work life filled with peace and contentment.

Compassion plus wisdom equals balance. Each day your actions, your words, and your behavior can make all the difference in the world and can bring you either joy or pain on the job. In Chapter 4, "Balance," you will see how you can live a sane and happy existence simply by "doing the right thing," and how your intuition can so inform your life that you can even remain spiritual in a nonspiritual environment.

Chapter 5, "Disciplined Attention," will explore how, by paying attention to every detail, this whole journey will bring you to the place where you can take what you've learned into your daily work life and use your work as a form of meditation. This in turn will bring you joy and satisfaction, both on the job and off. If you truly pay attention, you will discover that anything is possible.

Once you've explored inside yourself you will begin

to realize that attaining wisdom, or discovering the truth, is the only way you can transcend the roadblocks on the path to freedom. In Chapter 6, "As Things Are," you will see how the right attitude, along with understanding, can lead you to the wisdom you need in order to make decisions that work for you. You will see how this wisdom can bring you happiness, and how work and love are not mutually exclusive.

In the last chapter, "You're Already There," you will understand the paradox that while your work is never done, in any given moment it is complete and perfect just as it is. And so are you. This knowledge will help you to accept your life as it is given to you and *just be.*

We've all been told—promised, even—by society, parents, professionals, teachers that if we do what we love, then not only will we be happy but we'll also make plenty of money. Conventional wisdom tells us that if we do what we love, all good things will follow. And this might well be true. But fear or financial concerns and obligations keep many of us from taking a big risk. So we remain where we are, deeply disappointed and discontented. The good news is that in order to find happiness and satisfaction in your work, it isn't necessary to quit your job, sell your home and farm out the kids. It's only necessary to see that your priorities have been upside down. You need to learn to love the doing of whatever you happen to be doing at each and every moment. And rather than thinking that this will enslave you to work that you quite frankly would rather not be doing, think instead that it will both make you happy and make you free. Then, from a position of jubilant freedom, you will be able to do anything your heart desires, and everything you do will empower and embolden you. So rather than waiting to do what you love in order to be happy, be happy with what you're doing. And all the rest will fall into place.

# DISCOVERY

What do most of us long for? A happy, healthy life? Certainly. And if you feel that you're not yet living that, then it must follow that you are unhappy in some way. Once you acknowledge this, you usually make the connection that liberation from your suffering will bring the desired contentment, and so you long for that. It can become a vicious cycle: dissatisfaction → desire → happiness → longing → dissatisfaction. But liberation is possible, and here in the first three steps of this process you will learn about your cycle of frustration and what has prevented you from living happily, especially with the work you do.

Although it may be hard to look at the how and why, you cannot extract yourself from the pervasive dissatisfaction of your life until you do. Here in "Discovery" you will come to understand how you have been looking all your life for something that doesn't exist. What you thought was solid is constantly changing and moving—you along with it. But rather than being frightening, this truth can be reassuring. As you continue to make your way through these first three steps, as you confront the truth, you will slowly (or in some instances very quickly) realize that this truth will set you free. You are not a cliché, but sometimes your life is. This is neither bad nor good—it simply is.

Approach the work suggested here as you would a job that you love to do. Put everything you have into this work. Practice and see it as an opportunity to express your beliefs, your ideals, your inner truth. And then take this same approach to your life's work. What you learn here can be immediately transferred to your everyday work life. This is a practical, usable process, not a theoretical one.

Some of what you uncover may be difficult for your ego to accept. Do not judge or criticize what you discover. Instead, use it for your own benefit. Don't let it rule you. Know that you are in charge here and that it is for you (and not your ego) that you do this work.

By the time you get to "The Path" you will have a clearer picture of who you are, where you've come from and where you want to go. You will be ready to accept the challenges of this process, and your day-to-day work experience will begin to improve. You will spend more time in the events of the day rather than in yesterday or tomorrow. This alone, in a very concrete, experiential way, will usher in a new sense of peace and contentment. In "Discovery" you will learn how to be in harmony with the changing circumstances of your life and be comfortable with nothing permanent to hold on to. Your spirit will then be able to soar, and your work life will mirror this newfound strength and happiness.

But don't take my word for it. Discover this for yourself. Do these first three steps with thoroughness and see for yourself. What can be better than that?

*The First Step*

# UNDERSTANDING AND ACCEPTANCE

■

Have you ever noticed how people (perhaps even you) seem to hate change and yet always wish for it? This mood of dissatisfaction expresses itself in our lives and most especially in our work. How many people do you know who are satisfied with their work? How many people do you know who like what they do but hate their boss? Or vice versa? How about those who complain no matter what they're doing? We seem to always want things to change, yet when they do we don't handle it very well. Perhaps we direct our dissatisfaction toward our work because for us work doesn't have a human face; it is impersonal. There is no one person responsible. There is no one person capable of making the changes we want. There is no one person who can assure us that nothing will ever change. Perhaps we complain about our work because others do or because we always have or because it's safer to attack work than it is to look at the issues that really upset us.

And why do company mergers create such tremendous anxiety among all levels of employees? Because such an event is a loud, roaring signal that things are about to change. It brings us face-to-face with the fundamental reality that was simply dwelling beneath the surface prior to the announced merger: *change happens*. And when we dwell in the unknown—what will happen to us? will we lose our job? will our benefits be reduced? will we be asked to move?—we let our fears take control. We indulge our runaway anxiety. After all, we are merely pawns in the company's hands. But what we don't realize is that nothing has really changed except our awareness. Even prior to the merger announcement our work situation was precarious—there were no guarantees, no stability, no security in any position. Whatever the situation, we need to find stability within ourselves and go there each time the fear of losing something we have, or not getting something we want, arises. We must find our inner strength and know that whatever happens, we will remain intact— able to support our families and ourselves. The whims of our bosses, the fluctuations in the economy and the shifts in the demand for the product or service we offer are all out of our control. So we must firmly plant ourselves in the soil of spiritual groundedness and sway gently with the changing winds of time, knowing that none is strong enough to uproot us. We will survive, we will prosper, we will be happy so long as our roots are firmly imbedded in the solid rock of acceptance and understanding.

On a hot day many people walk around complaining about the heat, miserable and cranky because the weather doesn't suit them. These same people also complain when it's rainy and cold or simply not a picture-perfect day. What these people lack is an acceptance of what is and an understanding that they are not in control. There's an old Zen saying that you might want to write on a piece of paper and tack up over your desk or work station, or carry around with you, to remind you that you are not in charge:

*When it's cold, shiver. When it's hot, sweat.*

And not only are you not in charge of the weather, but you are also not in charge of company policy or how it gets executed or who your coworkers are. (Even if you are the boss who sets the company policy, you cannot control every little aspect of a dynamic organization.) So . . .

*When it's cold, shiver. When it's hot, sweat.*

Each time you look at it, and each time you hear yourself complaining about the weather or your job or your boss, let this saying remind you that the only way the weather, or anything else, will change is if you move to a different climate or when time takes its course. But before you make any drastic changes, consider that staying put and sweating or shivering might be the best answer. Moving away will not guarantee that the new situation will be more to your liking. Let this saying also remind you that while you may not be in charge of the weather, you are in charge of your reaction to it. And this is where you must look to understand why you are dissatisfied and what you can do about it. You must look to yourself.

You must first pay closer attention to the actual circumstances and come to an understanding of how and why things are the way they are. And sometimes you must learn to accept what is, without expecting any deeper understanding. This may sound obvious and simplistic, but the truth of your life may surprise you once you take a closer look.

So as you begin to look at yourself and your work life, keep in mind the following questions: *Is your work nature different and separate from your nature outside work? Is your job, your work, the cause of your dissatisfaction, or does the source lie elsewhere?* Write for a few minutes addressing these two questions. Then sit for a few minutes and reflect on what you've discovered about yourself. Perhaps nothing new will reveal itself yet. This is okay. Or perhaps these two simple questions will stimulate more confusion than you're ready to handle right now. This is okay too. Just breathe, relax and know that there is no right response. You are not expected to be anyplace but exactly where you are right now, in this moment. If you're confused, be confused.

After you've taken a few minutes to contemplate them, put these two questions aside and move on. Come back to them from time to time and pay attention to the shifts that take place as you learn more about yourself and your approach to work. Know that what you touch on now is the merest beginning. And keep in mind that more will be revealed as you move along in this process of discovery, toward a clearer understanding and acceptance of who you are and what work means in your life.

*The highest form of goodness is like water.*
*Because it benefits all things without competing*
*and has no trouble abiding in places that none would care*
*to be,*
*it comes close to the Way.*

*In dwelling, what matters is keeping close to the ground.*
*In thinking, what matters is simplicity.*
*In dealing with others, what matters is benevolence.*
*In speaking, what matters is sincerity.*
*In business, what matters is efficiency.*
*In activity, what matters is timeliness.*

*When you are true to yourself*
*and don't compare or compete,*
*you will live with honor.*

TAO TE CHING (#8)

# Things Change

Few of us deny that natural events in life—birth, death, illness and aging—cause us pain, grief and sorrow. We accept that these occurrences are natural, yet each time we encounter one we allow ourselves to suffer and rail against the injustice, the unfairness of the world. Time and time again we are confronted with our lack of control and the inevitability of change. When the winds of change subside, when things return to normal, we breathe a little easier and fool ourselves into thinking that this normal state is fixed, rigid and unchanging and that the catastrophic events are abnormal and infrequent. We hold on that much tighter to what we think of as our predictable everyday life, believing that our suffering is over for the time being, at least until the next catastrophe hits.

The very first thing we must do to find happiness (and isn't that what we all want?) in our work life or in any other area of our life is to come to terms not only with the fact that things change but with the fact that these changes—even the seemingly minor ones— cause us to be dissatisfied with ourselves, with our lives and with those around us. Here's an example of how it happens.

*We arrive at work one morning expecting to be met with our usual tasks, with the usual faces. Our boss greets us first thing and informs us that for the next three weeks everyone in the department will be working together in teams on a special project. This will mean working overtime and on weekends. We are teamed up with the one person in the department that we don't get along with. Rather than greeting this news with excitement (it's a challenging opportunity to use our skills, which could lead to recognition and promotion), we mope and complain. Our weekend plans are destroyed. We become angry and sullen both at work and at home. We make the next three weeks miserable for ourselves and everyone around us. We see no joy anywhere.*

We are all looking for certainty. And when we construct in our minds a vision of how things should be, of how they should play out, of the perfect scenario, we can't help but be disappointed, since the reality is always different. But we can help ourselves and lessen our disappointment by refraining from the mind constructs that will only lead us down the road to pain.

Here are some truths to consider:

*Change is inevitable.*
*Nothing is permanent.*

Intellectually we can all grasp these truths. We need only take a quick review of our lives, or for that matter the past week or day, to prove them. So if our mind agrees with these truths, and if we agree that it is our mind that regularly tries to convince us that they're not true, where does that leave us? Logically this conclusion would lead us to look elsewhere.

We must go to our spiritual self to fully grasp, understand and live with the truth that impermanence is the way of life and acceptance of that truth the only key that will release us from our suffering and dissatisfaction.

So where is our spirit located? Is it in our heart? Is it in our gut? Does it have a specific locale within our body? For the time being let's not worry about where our spiritual center is; let's just simply decide that it's not in our brain. Let's also agree that while our spiritual center is not in our mind, we might at some point need to engage our mind, once we begin to activate our spirit, to fully understand what is going on. But for now our practice will be pulling away from our mind's activity and breathing our way toward our spirit. Concentrate on the following exercise each time you feel your mind struggling for an answer:

---

*Breathe deeply. Concentrate only on your deep breath. Draw your breath as deeply into your tummy as possible. Imagine your center of gravity just below your belly button. Concentrate all of your energy there so that the activity of your mind falls away and you are centered in the middle of your body rather than in your head. Breathe, breathe and breathe some more. Breathe until your thoughts have quieted down. Breathe until your anxiety has abated. If you take the time to do this every day, you will soon know without a doubt where your spiritual center is. Your breath will guide you. Trust it. Don't listen to the chatter in your brain; it is only chatter. Listen to what your breath wants to say. You will know it when you hear it. Understanding will be yours in time.*

---

1. Write down everything that you are presently dissatisfied with in your work life, and write about how your work (and your dissatisfaction with it) spills over into the rest of your life to cause yet more dissatisfaction.

Some areas to think about:

Your boss
Your coworkers
The office environment
Your compensation package
Your commute
Your hours
The work itself

2. Write about what you would change to make it better, to make you happier.
3. Write about those things in your work/job that make you happy, that you wouldn't want changed.

Don't do anything with this information yet. Just sit with it and trust that you'll know what to do when the time comes. Or live with doubt. That's okay too.

---

# Follow the Leader

In Western culture we are conditioned to praise the individual, on one hand, and to be like everyone else, on the other. As children, we are taught how to fit in, follow the rules and play as a member of a team. But it is always the outstanding individual who gets the special attention and accolades. We are told to follow the leader, and many of us vie for that coveted front spot. And if we are too far behind or too shy or simply not aggressive enough to get noticed or to fight for the front row, we often begin to resent the person in the spotlight and grow up feeling "less than." The effects of such conditioning are not always obvious. By the time we become aware of these influences they are such an integral part of who we have become that we can't easily isolate them. But if we learn to pay attention in the here and now, we can heighten our awareness and lessen their impact.

Because modern society extols and honors the successful individualist, many of us feel left behind. Even in team sports it is the exception rather than the rule that the team is praised first. Most likely one or two individuals on the team are credited with the team's success. Michael Jordan is a perfect example. Granted, he was an extraordinary athlete. And most people know that without his teammates he could not have done what he did half as well. But the discrepancy between his and his teammates' fame and money was staggering. Yet we accept it as the way of the modern world and rationalize that he deserved such riches because he was gifted and entertained us. We try to pretend that it doesn't bother us. But the seeds of greed and envy may be sown when a coworker gets a promotion and raise and leaves us behind, or when we meet someone who loves his or her work, makes more money than we do and has a happy, contented love relationship. We can't help but compare ourselves. We might see these people as the chosen ones, the leaders, the ones destined to get all the breaks. We become angry and embittered. Most likely we are not even aware of how these feelings combine to color our perception. We simply know that we are dissatisfied. All of this bitterness can turn inward, sowing self-hatred. Little do we know how these feelings prevent us from loving anything or anyone, or how they cause us to look toward others to save us, and when they don't, to blame them for our condition.

So the first thing that we have to look at is what is going on internally—not for your neighbor, your co-workers or Michael Jordan, but for you. The second thing to understand is that the externals, in the end, mean nothing. They contribute nothing to our spiritual under-standing of the world (except as they might offer to teach us something) and only work to separate us from each other. When all the externals are stripped away we are left with what makes us human, and in that state we are all equal under the laws of the universe. And it is with this raw material that we can make a difference in the world. We have some control over how we use the raw materials we've been given (our hearts and minds, for instance) and if we can learn to keep our focus on this, on our own individual selves, then we can find hap-piness in our work, in our lives. We can learn to con-tribute to the world what we were meant to contribute, without resentment. We can learn to appreciate what we have, acknowledge that it is enough, and be grateful for it.

If you're thinking that all of this sounds too lofty and spiritual and has nothing to do with making a living and liking your job, I will pose a challenge and make you a promise. If you are willing to suspend for a short time your traditional notions of what making a living means, what your job or your work or your career is or should be, and what money can do for you, and if you approach the material in this book with sincerity and an open mind, taking the suggested steps and doing all of the exercises, I promise that you will find happiness in your daily work life and know instinctively how to handle the challenges that life presents. All lingering self-hatred and resentment of others will disappear. But—and this is where you come in—you must do the work. No one else can do it for you. No one else is responsible for your interpretation of your life. You must be honest with yourself through this process. You must stand up and move to the front row of your life. There is only one you. You are the leader here. You are the only one who inhabits your unique world. You are what matters, your life is what matters, and you can make a difference in your life. So show up for yourself and take a risk to be fully and truly you. Stand tall in your own shoes. Walk in your own footsteps. And in the end—or even right now, in this moment—you will see that you are better than no one else and no one else is better than you. You are just you. And while we really have no other choice but to be ourselves, being aware of being ourselves takes some courage. So be brave, be aware, be diligent. If you take it one step at a time, one small moment at a time, one breath at a time, your life will open up and you will begin to see it as the miracle that it is.

Congratulations for being ready. You've chosen yourself. You are in the front row, following yourself as the leader of your life.

Write an appraisal of your current work situation. Be specific. Be honest. Be thorough. Don't rush through this. Take as long as you need to complete this exercise.

1. Make two lists, one of the pros of your job, one of the cons. Here's an example:

PROS                          CONS
Location is ideal             Dislike my boss
Subsidized cafeteria          Bored much of the time
Casual dress code on          Lousy compensation
Fridays                       package

2. Write about a recent accomplishment or a daily task that you do that you are most proud of in your work.
3. Write about something you've done or have neglected to do at work most recently that you are least proud of.
4. Describe how you think your coworkers view you and your contribution at work.
5. Describe how you see yourself at work. Try to draw a balanced picture—don't judge too harshly, don't praise too highly. How are you as an employee? How are you as a boss? Would you want to work for you?
6. Write two job descriptions, one to include what you think the responsibilities of your specific job are, the other to include what you believe your boss

or the company thinks your responsibilities are. How much in sync are these two views? How have the differences evolved? What is your investment in nurturing these differences? How much of a role does your ego or pride take in keeping your vision and the company's vision separate?

---

As you begin this process—and keep in mind that it is a process—and especially as you write down the details of your life, the details that up to now have only been in your head and heart, you will get in touch with a reality that has previously been clouded by emotions, and you will begin to identify the negative emotions responsible. Some of these will include pride, jealousy, desire, ignorance and enmity.

Go back over what you've written and try to get in touch with the feelings that are aroused as you think about your current work situation and the people you work with. If you can't name a feeling, try to describe it. Write a list of these feelings and what they're attached to.

As you sit quietly each day accept what you've been feeling and look deeply into why you're feeling these things. Without denying your feelings and without grabbing on and being carried away by them, just look, just observe, just pay attention. After you've sat with them write again about what else came up. Go back the next day and sit with them again. Write about them again. Keep breathing and learning about yourself, about what grabs you, what motivates you, what scares you.

Pray that you will be released from the control that your emotions have over you. Don't judge yourself. Forgive yourself for being human. Remember: simplicity, patience, compassion. As you are working on this exercise pay more attention while you're at work, and as emotions come up on the job try to take a short prayer and meditation break. Breathe your way through the day, through the emotions that get stirred up and then move into the reality of your life. For that is where you must be in order to make a change, if change is what is needed.

## Our Ordinariness

Do you compartmentalize your life? Do you have a work persona that is different from your leisure persona or the persona you bring to your intimate relationships? Who is the self that you bring to work each day?

Let's examine for a moment the various elements that combine to create the idea we have of this self that we bring to work.

First, each of us has a physical form, a body, that has (if we're lucky) five sense organs (eyes, ears, nose, tongue, body) and a mental organ, our mind.

Second, each of us goes out into the world with these six faculties and experiences physical and mental sensations through them, that is, we feel things.

Third, these six faculties then combine to give us our perception of the world, what we think.

Fourth, we develop, condition and control these six faculties as we go out into the world. How we choose to use them—our volition—determines how we get along in the world.

Fifth, we, our selves, are not separate from these faculties; they merely combine to give us our idea of self. Thus we become conscious or aware of visible things through our eyes, of sound through our ears, of scent through our nose, of taste through our tongue, of tangible objects through our touch, of thought through our mind. Our sensations and perceptions carry us to an awareness of the world, to consciousness.

So we have these five states—form, feeling, thought, volition, consciousness—that, along with our five senses and mental faculties, combine to give us our personality, our sense of self, our being. We respond physically and mentally to the conditions around us. And if we were not ordinary humans, we would simply accept whatever happened. We would see things for what they are and know that we are each a mere part of the whole, that everything and everyone is interconnected and that there really is no separated, individuated self. There is merely a perception, an idea of self. We would be blissfully happy no matter what was going on around us, living from our innate nature.

But who of us can claim to have such an acceptance and understanding of the world? Not many, I dare say, though there may be a few. But it is possible to move ever closer to this. We are capable of it. And since we do have control over our senses and mental faculties, we can move in the right direction, especially once we grasp the concept that there is no self outside of these six faculties moving us along. And even before we fully grasp this (for it takes time and practice to realize it) we can take steps to form a clearer understanding of who and what we really are.

Please keep in mind that it is not easy to embrace our innate nature. It cannot be conceived of or imagined in the usual ways. It is something beyond explanation. We cannot think or feel our way to an understanding of it. It is not what some people call our soul. It is not God. It is not ego. It does not have a form. Our five conditioned states—form, feeling, thought, volition, consciousness—are constantly in flux, are ever changing. Our innate nature doesn't change. Our six faculties—seeing, hearing, smelling, tasting, touching, thinking—never remain the same from one moment to the next. Our innate nature is consistent and constant. Yet this nature has no substance. It cannot be thought into existence. It just is. It is stillness, though that doesn't define it. It is ever present. Because of that we have a chance to discover it, to uncover it, to become aware of it, to awaken to it. All of life has it. All of nonlife has it. It is the thread that holds everything together. It is the spaces between everything. It is silence. It is emptiness. It is nothing. No thing. No form, no feeling, no thought, no volition, no consciousness. It is what will ease our suffering and bring us joy. No eyes, no ears, no nose, no tongue, no body, no mind. There is no easy way to understand this. Relax. You needn't try to find it. If you are patient, if you truly want to be happy and if you do the work that's necessary, it will find you. And when it does, you will know it—and you'll know how near it has always been. Relax, for you are in it now.

So how does all this relate to work, to loving your work and doing what you love? Well, before you can address the outside issues you have to spend a little time inside getting to know yourself. You need to become acquainted with whom you bring to work each day. And even if you doubt that there's a connection to happiness at work, do the exercises anyway. This work will benefit your "real" work. I guarantee it. And you may even start to question what the real work in your life is.

---

1. Write about your six faculties (seeing, hearing, smelling, tasting, touching, thinking) and how they inform your view of the world; your awareness of people, places and things; your behavior; your thoughts and feelings.
2. Which of the six do you rely on most heavily to make your way in the world? Which brings you the most joy? The most pain? Describe the joy and pain that each brings you. Which is your favorite?
3. Describe your attitudes and feelings about work, first in general and then specifically about your current job. Where do these feelings come from? Are they based in reality? Can you see that sometimes your feelings are just feelings and not the facts? Can you allow yourself to feel your feelings without carrying any judgments of yourself or

others with them? Can you forgive yourself for being an ordinary human with feelings? Can you just accept the feelings as yours and not expect the world to conform to them?

---

For the next week pay special attention to your five states and six faculties. When you see something, ask yourself who is it that's doing the seeing. Who is it that hears, tastes, smells and touches? Who thinks your thoughts? Don't be concerned about finding the correct answer, or any answer for that matter. Be content just to ask the questions. Hone your awareness of yourself.

Take some time each day to find a quiet spot to sit alone and just breathe. As you concentrate on your breath, listen for the answers. Listen with your whole body. When a thought takes you away from your breath concentration, ask yourself who had the thought in the first place, if you were concentrating on breathing, and who then realized that you were having that thought. Maybe there's an answer, maybe not. For now it's enough to be asking the questions. Each time you become aware of some discomfort in your body, ask yourself who is experiencing the pain. Then return to your breath. Just breathe. And swim in the ordinariness of your being.

# Expectations

"Expectation is a premeditated resentment!" When I heard someone exclaim this many years ago, it reached my gut and exploded there, sending shock waves of truth to every part of my being. It gave me a keener and deeper understanding of the first two words I remember hearing from my spiritual teacher: "Expect nothing!" Yet when his incantation—"Expect nothing. Expect nothing. Expect nothing"—first reached my ears, I didn't have the slightest idea what it meant. My life up to that point had been all about expectations, so filled with them that I thought expectations were not only normal but obligatory. I thought that having expectations meant that I was engaged in my life and that I cared about the course it took. I thought that having expectations was the only way I could achieve my goals. And yet I didn't really think so much about expectations at all. I simply knew I had them, especially when I was asked to expect nothing. And it wasn't until then that I was able to link my disappointments in life to the expectations I had. Today I know that disappointment is always preceded by an expectation. Every feeling of hurt, any mood of anger, every judgment, each criticism and all frustrations are the results of expectation. And these expectations are not always clearly in view. But whenever there is emotional irritation the source can invariably be found in the wellspring of expectation, a source that never seems to run dry.

From something as simple as being disappointed in a new movie because it didn't live up to the hype—that is, we *expected* it to be fabulous—to the hurt and anger generated by our partner because he/she didn't live up to the promise we thought we'd been given, our expectations cause us pain. Expectations = disappointment = resentment. We set ourselves up for the inevitable fall when we have an expectation. And though the fallout on a personal level is often hard to take—many of us suffer physical and mental breakdown when the unexpected happens—as a society, nothing seems to truly shock us anymore. Hence we have all come to *expect* to be disappointed in other people. As a result, many of us walk around with resentments, unaware that the real cause stems from our own expectations—expectations of ourselves, expectations of others, expectations of our jobs. And all these expectations emanate from fear. All our disappointments and all our resentments and anguish can be traced back to their source: fear of not getting what we want and losing what we have. Our expectations were not fulfilled. We did not get what we expected to get. The scenario did not unfold as we imagined it. We lost something we expected to have forever. But nothing is forever. And, paradoxically, once we accept this we can forever be rid of the pain and grief that our expectations cause us.

Expectation rooted in fear is probably the most potent source of our emotional pain and suffering, especially when it comes to our work life. If you have a resentment, no doubt you expected something that didn't happen. And once you become aware that expectations lead to resentments, then the realization that you are the agent of your own suffering is not far behind. This truth is not something that is easy to swallow or even understand. And it will take time to get used to the idea that your expectations (which begin and end with you) not only interfere with your spiritual progress but also interfere with your having healthy intimate relationships and strong, constructive work relationships—indeed, relationships of any kind.

And here's another stunning truth that may initially shock you and perhaps even seem ludicrous: hopes and dreams fall into the same category as expectations, that is, they are spoilers of the truth and roadblocks to spiritual freedom. Hopes and dreams invariably carry an expectation on their tail, even if we take pains to avoid tacking any expectation onto them. It is difficult to stop short of expectation when we harbor hopes and dreams, because as soon as we begin to describe to ourselves what we dream and hope for, we lock ourselves into the scenario. And if what we end up with looks different, we experience disappointment and resentment—against the world, against someone else, against a situation, against an organization, even against God. So if you feel resentment or anger toward someone, before expressing it and before it gets out of control, do a little inner search. Look for the root of it. Look for the expectation that spawned it. And then if you work on expunging the expectation, the resentment will have nothing to hold on to and will fade away and lose power over you.

Now, all of this does not mean that you can't have goals, dreams and aspirations. But it does mean that you cannot afford to attach any expectation to any of it. So if ridding your life of expectation promises to reduce disappointment and resentment, why not give it a try? All you have to lose is something you'd rather not have anyway.

Let's now examine the expectations you've nurtured all your life in relation to your work. And then let's look at how even the smallest expectation on any given day can get in your way.

---

1. When you were little did you have dreams, ideas or expectations of what you would be when you grew up? If so, write about them. Then write about where you are today and how this differs from your childhood vision. Are you where you imagined yourself to be? Does this please you? How do you feel? Write about all of this.

2. Now write about the career expectations you had or didn't have as a young adult. Write about your parents' expectations of you and how they meshed with your own vision. Were there internal and external conflicts? Write about them.

3. Write about the expectations you have today regarding your work—expectations of you, your boss, your coworkers, your company.

4. At the end of the day review in your mind and in writing the disappointments you experienced at work (big and small) and the resentments that

were activated. Trace each one to an expectation (there's bound to be one) and examine that. Then practice letting go of the expectation. Do this exercise as often as you can (every day, once a week) and don't expect anything to happen. Simply do the exercise.

---

You might be asking yourself, "If I eliminate expectations, hopes and dreams from my life, what's left?" Good question. And the answer is a simple one. *Now*. That's what's left. Now. This moment. The everlasting, wonderfully rich present. Expectation projects us into the future. When we finally do get there, it's always different from what we imagined. But if we stay in the present and live in anticipation of the future, then we are right where we are, we have no illusions, and we can't possibly be disappointed. Which means a life free of resentments.

As with any new skill, it takes some practice to master staying in the moment. We cannot expect to be proficient at eliminating expectation from our life simply because we want to and believe in the promise that we will be free of resentments and disappointments. After all, we have years of bad habits to wash away. But we can practice each day, each moment. Before too long you'll acquire a sixth sense that will tell you when you're crossing the thin line between anticipation and expectation, and you'll be able to rein it in before it moves into disappointment. So be patient, practice and enjoy the possibility of each moment.

# Blaming

When something goes wrong (and something always does if "wrong" means "not as expected"), how often do you step up and take responsibility? Or do you see it as blame and try to turn the spotlight away from you and onto something or someone else? Most of us are taught at a very young age to turn away from blame so that we might escape punishment. Even if it was only a simple talking-to, we wanted to avoid anything that smacked of shame. So we learned to point the finger away from ourselves. But shouting "He did it" or "I had nothing to do with it" or "I wasn't involved" or "If she had done so-and-so, this wouldn't have happened" not only demeans us but causes others to take a defensive stand. We excel at placing blame and often lack the inner strength to apologize, to make amends, to admit when we're wrong. We see our professional relationships as just not important and intimate enough to work on and improve.

And even if the people around us—our bosses, our coworkers, our staff—behave poorly and create an atmosphere of tension and mistrust, it is not our job to point to them to justify our own bad behavior. Their bad behavior is none of our business. All we need be concerned with is our own behavior. At the end of each day ask yourself the following questions:

*Did I mind my own business at work today?*
*Was I critical of others and their performance?*

*Did I blame someone else for something I wasn't able to accomplish?*
*How much time did I spend with my coworkers today?*
*Is it important to have open and honest relationships with these people?*

Granted, we must often rely on others at work to get our job done well. But rather than getting tripped up by someone else's slack, go on to the next thing. Don't let your anger and self-righteousness stop you in your tracks and allow you to slack off as well. That would not be their fault. That would be your fault. Then continue to ask yourself throughout and at the end of each day:

*Did I contribute my share at work today?*
*Did I allow someone else's behavior to affect my productivity? And if so, did I blame them?*
*Did I confront problems head on, or did I grouse quietly and complain to others who had no power to alleviate the problem?*

What about when someone you work with blatantly blames you for some mishap? How do you handle it? Does it turn into a battle of "It's your fault," "No, it's your fault"? Chances are it's nobody's fault, so trying to pin it on someone is a waste of everyone's time. And so what if it is someone's fault? How does placing blame rectify the situation? Instead, try this: insist that no one is to blame and suggest that you all simply look at the problem and decide together how it might be remedied. If this doesn't

WORK FROM THE INSIDE OUT

work, take the blame yourself, even if it's not your fault (unless, of course, this would mean losing your job, but generally it's never that serious). This admission will usually take the wind out of everyone's sails. There will no longer be a target for their frustration. Given a real live target—you—they will be willing to let it go and move on to solve the problem. You might be surprised how people will actually look up to you after you admit blame. It is so rarely done that they will be in shock and not know how to handle it. Not only will you be safe from harm but you'll feel like a million bucks, and you'll all be able to get back to the business of doing business, no longer distracted by the question of who's to blame.

This tendency to blame, to take the focus off ourselves, takes many different forms. If we're unhappy in our work, we look around to see what or who is culpable. Rarely do we look at ourselves. We might look at the work itself as boring, unstimulating, enervating. Or we look at our superiors, decide that we could do a better job than they are doing and then become resentful and unproductive because of the inequities in financial compensation. Or we blame the company, the guys upstairs, for the state of things down where we are. There is no real target for our frustrations, just the amorphous *them*, and everyone walks around demoralized and inefficient. We'll look at the we/they syndrome later on—for now let's just look at the issues of the work itself. I believe that each one of us can find work that is suitable to our skills and interests and can find satisfaction in our daily work routine. (You'll learn later how routine in our lives is not a bad thing.) So if your current work bores you and holds little stimulation for you, you must look at why you're where you are, how you got there in the first place and where you might want to be instead. Rather than complaining, blaming and being miserable, look at the realities and consider how much of your misery comes from within rather than from the job itself. Ask yourself the following questions:

*How did I land here in this particular job?*
*What attracted me to it in the first place?*
*Are there any aspects of it that still interest me?*
*Putting aside the issue of money [we'll cover that in detail later], what satisfaction do I find in the work itself?*

Whether you can see it yet or not, know that it was your choice to be where you are; only you are responsible for that choice, and only you can change it if it needs changing. But before you make any big changes, try approaching your daily routine with a different mind-set. Focus on the positive. Focus on those aspects of the job that once gave you pleasure. Bring all of your attention to each task, each moment of every day, even the unpleasant ones. Try not to judge these tasks as unpleasant; approach them simply as tasks to be done, as something to be accomplished, as part of your job. Be grateful for the good and bad elements of your job. In adopting such an attitude you might find that the unpleasantness seeps away. You may never become fully enraptured with every tiny aspect, but your overall appreciation and fulfillment will increase if you bring all your attention to each detail, moment by moment. And then when the blaming and complaining stop, you will be in a purer state and hence in a better position to decide whether you should stay or go, whether it was the job or you, whether you really like your job or not. And then you will have a clearer sense of what is right for you, of what fits with your natural inclinations, of what keeps you happy.

Now, what of those people above you who are responsible for supervising your work and passing judgment on it (or those who have the jobs you covet)? You may be smarter than your boss, more talented and more creative. It seems to happen all the time. People are always complaining about their bosses and their lack of talent and understanding. But consider this: if you are focused on what you don't have (your boss's job) or what you should have (your boss's money) or on other people's performance, then maybe you're not doing your job as well as you could. Perhaps there's a quality in your boss that you've been missing. Perhaps you could look for the positive, if you must look there at all. Or maybe for a while you can turn your focus sharply onto your own job and spend all your concentration there rather than allow yourself to be distracted by others.

Ask yourself these questions:

> *Do I want my boss's job?*
> *Do I serve my boss as well as I could?*
> *Do I help my bosses do their jobs as well as they can?*
> *What is my role as employee?*

*Do I undermine my position in the company? How do I do this?*

*Do I let my envy and resentments interfere with my own performance?*

*At the end of the day am I proud of the job I did or am I focused on what others didn't do?*

*Is there anyone in the company to look up to, to admire and emulate? What qualities does this person have that I could adopt and start exhibiting?*

Spend some time writing about your tendency to blame others. If issues from the past come up as you write about today, don't ignore them, but don't get lost there either. Acknowledge them, accept them and let them go. Then bring yourself into the present, as an adult, and know that you are responsible for your behavior today, no matter what your past. So spend some time getting to know yourself by writing about your behavior at work, your relationships with the people there, and what you can do to change things *today*. Spend some quiet time by yourself absorbing your discoveries and letting them go. Breathe them into your body, own them and breathe them away. Clear your mind each day by writing about what happened and how it affected you. Then sit in the quiet of your breath and understand that you have choices, that you can change you. This understanding will then ripple through your life in unexpected ways. You do what you can do and then watch what happens. Enjoy the uncertainty and mystery of it all. Breathe and appreciate things as they are.

# Security in Being the Victim

You are not separate from your life. Life and the way you live it are not two different things. You do not stand outside your life and watch it happen to you. Your life *is* you. There is no you beyond your life, beyond what is happening in your life. So throw aside for now the idea that you are merely a pawn, a victim in someone else's plan for your life. Whether or not you see it now, you are participating in your life. You are not a victim of circumstances.

And so with work. You are your work. There is not you and then your work. You are not separate from your work. (You disappear and become one with your work.) Work is not simply something you do so that you can live your life, something that must be gotten out of the way so that you can move on to the important things. Work is your life, or part of your life anyway, and is not separate from the rest of it, is not something that doesn't matter, that has no merit, that is just something to get through, to endure. Work in this day and age gets a bad rap. It is said matter-of-factly, as though it were a well-known truism, that no one gets to the end of their life, looks back and says, "I wish I had worked more and harder." Well, why not? (Addiction to work, work as merely an escape from life, is something else entirely; we'll look at that later.) Work is an estimable act. Work gives us dignity. Work affords us many gifts. And yet there are probably more people like my father than not. My father detested going to work each day and imparted to none of his eight children the value of work; he could not wait to retire, to be done with work. The problem was, he died before his planned early retirement. He waited for his work to end before he could begin to live, but he died before he had that chance. He, like many people, felt victimized by his work. He felt he had no choices. He became a prisoner of his own mind, not of his employer.

We all have choices. And until we recognize and admit that we have chosen our current situation, we will not be free to choose something else. There are no limits placed on us except those we place on ourselves. Our bosses, our companies, our paychecks do not dictate the rules of the work game. We only decide that they do.

And this doesn't mean that we should all walk away from our jobs if we feel victimized by them. This doesn't mean that we should act out at work, asserting our power. This doesn't mean that we can ignore the duties and responsibilities of our job and begin to do things our way. What it does mean is that we can begin to assess how we got where we are, what we're doing there and what we want going forward. We can take a realistic look at our employers and decide if they truly are our oppressors. We can move away from the security that comes with being a victim. And we can take responsibility for where we are and what we're doing.


Let's look at Walter. His work life exemplifies how easy it is to get stuck in the role of victim and delude ourselves into thinking that life happens to us, that we neither make nor have any choice in the direction that it takes.

Walter fell into his career after college, the way so many of us do. He liked his field well enough and moved along in it quite nicely. At first he was content to be there, and he quickly got attached to his paycheck and the other perks of full-time employment. In the back of his mind he had plans for his future, which included his real life's work. He got married, had a few kids, and moved up in the company. He did his job well, got along with his coworkers and superiors and settled into a middle management position. There was some autonomy in his job, which suited Walter because he hated to be told what to do and how to do it. As the years went by, Walter's world got smaller and smaller and his work options became less and less—at least in his own mind. When Walter reached his mid-forties and found himself with the same company, in the same job, he looked around and wondered how such a fate had come to befall him. Walter had become a disgruntled complainer. He continued to do his job well enough that the company had no reason to get rid of him, but he began to undermine the company's efforts. Walter complained to anyone who would listen, inside and outside the company—he had contact with representatives of many businesses that serviced his company—about how stupid and irresponsible upper management was, about how they were destroying the company, about how he was only doing their bidding and if someone didn't like the work he was producing then they should take it up with them and not him. When asked why he didn't just leave and find a situation more to his liking, Walter would enumerate the reasons: he had already put in a lot of time with the company and didn't want to risk his seniority, the company would never fire him, his family needed this security and he owed it to them, he was too old to start over in a new career, he couldn't afford it, he didn't have the energy, he didn't know what he would do. So he stayed, and stays on to this day, miserable and cranky most of the time. Because Walter feels like a victim, he is a victim. But his company is not the victimizer. Walter himself is.

---

1. Write a narrative work history of how you got to where you are. Start with your first job. Describe how you viewed each job, what your work dreams and aspirations were and still are, why you made the choices you made, what you liked and disliked about each job. Notice if a distinct pattern begins to emerge as you look at the whole. Write about this.

2. Do you feel that you are a victim of society, your employer, your job, your upbringing? Describe why and how this makes you feel. Then look at your part in it. What can you begin to do to change these feelings, to take charge of your own work life? If you don't know yet, write about that and the possible frustration it causes you. Be

patient; in time you will know. Accept where you are today, right now, in this process.

---

# Seeing Things as They Are

At the age of thirty-five, Karen was finally in the job of her dreams, having worked very hard to get there. With the help of a good therapist, a few strong women mentors, a loving family and a close group of friends, Karen was able to give up a successful and financially rewarding career that she decided was just not suited to her personality, and move into a potentially less lucrative career that promised to make her happier. She had many family and financial responsibilities and the change was risky, but she took the plunge and never looked back. For five years it was smooth sailing. Her new work environment was friendly and the work itself satisfied her in a way nothing else had. Even though she made less money, Karen hardly noticed. The joy she got from her everyday work life made it all worthwhile. And she knew that the future held the possibility of earning more money. Financial reward was not her first priority anymore, but she was happy to have that to look forward to. And she was so pleased to finally be in a job she loved that almost nothing else mattered.

Karen's maturity and previous work experience won her great latitude in her new profession. With respect and admiration from her boss, Frank, there also came a great deal of autonomy. Being a self-motivator, Karen sparkled in her new job, and many previously hidden talents rose to the surface. She got along well with her coworkers, and aside from the normal and mundane petty complaints, Karen's job satisfaction couldn't have been greater.

And then, as happens, things changed. Her boss was promoted and replaced with someone from outside. This new boss, Sondra, was ten years her junior. By this time Karen was forty years old and only five years into her new profession. Observing her new boss made Karen feel old and inexperienced. Add to that Sondra's hands-on management style, and Karen began to feel stifled and then threatened. She slipped into some of her old habits. She complained to anyone who would listen, at work and at home, about her new boss. She sought out other disgruntled employees to commiserate with. Her manner toward Sondra was curt and passively hostile. She began to romanticize her old job and miss the money. She felt abused and underpaid. Needless to say, Karen's job satisfaction metamorphosed overnight into job dissatisfaction, and there was no consoling her. Six months after her new boss arrived, Karen's annual salary review and job performance evaluation were due. Sondra gave Karen poor grades and no merit increase in salary. Karen was at first devastated and then livid. She had been hoping for a sizable pay increase. But this was also a huge wake-up call, and luckily she heard it.

Karen took a few days away from work to evaluate her situation. She went on long walks, she meditated, she wrote about her feelings, she talked to people. From experience, Karen knew that she needed to look at herself, her boss and her work situation in a nonjudgmental, honest way. She was aware that her ego and its compare-and-compete strategy had clouded her vision and tainted her actions. Her self-righteous, arrogant behavior became obvious even to her. She reviewed her career paths and was able to discern a pattern of behavior. With the arrival of her new boss, Karen's world had changed, and not to her liking. She had begun to voice disdain for her job even though deep down she knew this wasn't the truth. And although she had slandered Sondra by talking of her incompetence and inexperience, she also knew this wasn't true. So when Karen was finally able to be honest with herself and see things as they really were, she had to admit that she loved her work, that her boss wasn't really so bad and that she had behaved horribly. She refused to judge herself; she only wanted to make things right and start enjoying her work again.

So on Monday morning Karen went to Sondra and owned up to her behavior, without shame. She suggested a reevaluation in three months in order to give herself a chance to show Sondra her other side. Karen went into this meeting with humility and no expectations. Sondra agreed to give Karen another chance and a new evaluation was scheduled.

Karen didn't regain the autonomy she had had with Frank, and she interacted with Sondra more often than was her liking, but she began to do her job the way her new boss preferred. She learned some new things, she was able to see Sondra's merits as a boss—and she still loved her work. She treasured even more than before the hours spent alone at her desk working on the task in front of her. Karen has since become grateful for this uncomfortable experience because she now knows herself better and is a more productive worker as a result. As she likes to say, "I was humiliated into humility. And I'm much better off for it."

So seeing things as they are rather than how we wish them to be, even if it means eating humble pie, is a more honest, truthful and in the end happier way of being. This state of awareness without judgment is not easy to attain, conditioned as we are to being dissatisfied. But when we do succeed, even once, we break the cycle of our suffering and begin to understand how we can surely move away from what was and into what is.

---

1. Choose one small aspect of your job that causes you dissatisfaction.
2. Step outside of it and, without judgment, describe it.
3. Now try to see it just for what it is (divorcing yourself from it for the moment). It is what it is and cannot be anything else. If you can get to this, then you will be on your way to a clear understanding of your unhappiness.
4. Now describe the emotions you attach to it that cause you grief.

5. Write about how it and your reaction to it are separate and distinct.

6. Over the course of the next week, start to change the way you relate to this aspect of your job. Experiment with various alternatives and see how each one makes you feel. Write about it as you go along, and at week's end notice if anything at all has shifted. Then write about that.

7. If you manage to change your relationship with this aspect of your job, observe and write about how your old approach affected other aspects of your job and how those may also have changed during this process.

---

# We All Want to Be Happy

We can be happy, even at work. But first we have to come to a truthful, nonjudgmental understanding of why we're unhappy. It's easy enough to recognize our unhappiness, our discontent and our dissatisfaction with work. The hard part is truly understanding it and then beginning the process of learning how to change the way we relate to our unhappiness. For only then can we transform it into its opposite: happiness.

So let's take a moment to review what you did in this first step toward understanding.

1. You identified the elements of your work that cause you dissatisfaction and how these feelings

seep into other areas of your life. You also identified those aspects of work that make you happy.

2. You made a balanced assessment of your current job—the pros, the cons, your contribution to it and where you might be lacking.

3. You appraised your personality, your thoughts and feelings, and looked at how you move through your world with your unique take on things.

4. You reviewed your self- and career expectations and noticed the disappointment attached to them.

5. You began to observe yourself in your daily work routine and how you might be contributing to your own dissatisfaction by taking the focus off yourself and placing it elsewhere, in either blame, envy or anger.

6. You looked at your work history and uncovered the pattern you wove.

7. Then you began to see things as they are by stepping outside those aspects of your work that cause you dissatisfaction and observing without judgment these elements and your reaction to them.

In order to fully and objectively understand our work life, it is important to have a clear picture of not only what pleases us but also what pains us, and then to see clearly where we fit into the scheme. As we learned, one crucial aspect to this step of understanding is the notion of impermanence. The sooner we grasp this truth, the sooner we will reach a permanent state of joy. Don't let this seeming paradox bog you down. For if we accept that change is inevitable, that from one moment to the next nothing is exactly the same and that no matter how hard we try we cannot fix anything or anyone, including ourselves, into a static frame, then we are on our way to seeing clearly and exactly how things are. This realization will lead you to the happiness you seek.

You may be having a lot of feelings about all of this right now. This is natural, especially if you fearlessly and honestly completed these first-step exercises. But do not be discouraged. All of this work is necessary if you want to love what you do and do what you love. This will lead to a clear understanding *without judgment* of you and your relationship to work. The sooner you get to this understanding, the sooner your work life will be transformed. And in place of fantasy and illusion, or delusion and denial, your work life will be grounded in a reality that will bring you true happiness.

> *In dealing with the perplexities of body and mind*
> *can you create harmony between them?*
> *As you concentrate on your breath*
> *can you become as supple as a child?*
> *In polishing the mirror of your mind*
> *can you keep it free of impurities?*
> *Without being sly and cunning*
> *can you love people and lead them?*

When it comes to matters of life and death
can you let events take their course?
Even as your understanding grows
can you return to not-knowing?

It gives birth and nurtures,
It has but doesn't possess.
It gives generously without expectation,
It takes care but doesn't control.
Such is called the supreme virtue.

TAO TE CHING (#10)

*The Second Step*

# SEEING CLEARLY
# AND LETTING GO

■

In a flash, in the blink of an eye, in one moment the dissatisfaction we experience in our work life can be transformed into deep satisfaction. All the components necessary for a fulfilling life are present right now. We are already there, fully actualized. But most of us cannot see it, let alone experience it. So we must look at what's blocking us, why it is that we cannot step off the treadmill we're on and learn to see our lives from a different perspective—say, standing still. It is not easy, and few people would call this step a fun one. Many people give up when they begin to encounter what this step brings out. It may seem that we're only going deeper into our dissatisfaction and exacerbating our pain. If this begins to happen to you, skip this section and move on rather than give up. You will have to come back to it, however, and when you finally complete it you will have a deeper understanding of the causes of your dissatisfaction and the means to eliminate it. But if it's too much for you right now, move on and return when you're ready.

We can sum up in one word the ultimate cause of all our unhappiness, dissatisfaction and disappointment: desire. Once we begin to crave something, we set in motion a destructive cycle of desire, attachment and ultimately hatred. In this section we will explore our desires in detail and learn how they contribute to our unhappiness.

At this point some people experience a lot of fear and want to turn away. This reaction is normal. Determination is all you need here to learn the truth that will liberate you. And you don't have to stop wanting things. You simply have to learn how to detach from the wanting and the getting so that you can enjoy what you have with a pure heart.

As you proceed keep in mind that all you need to do once you identify the cause or source of your dissatisfaction is to discard it. Destroy it. Stop it. This will become clearer as you go along. It is a simple principle, which will become clear if you complete the following exercises.

---

1. Write about a recent experience of wanting something and then getting it. First, write about how the thirst, the desire for this thing made you feel, about how not having it kept you in a dissatisfied state and about how the thought of having it made you feel.

2. Then write about how satisfying it was to get that thing and how long that satisfaction lasted. Did the acquisition of this thing live up to your expec-

tations? How long did it satisfy you? Did getting it quench your thirst or did your desire then move on to some other thing?

3. Now write about a recent experience of sorely wanting something and then not getting it.

4. Then separate in your mind the desire for this thing and the thing itself, and write about your feelings toward both.

---

Can you see how in both cases it was the desire for something that caused the pain? Getting the desired thing might temporarily assuage our dissatisfaction, but it never completely eliminates it. There is always something else to want. So the only answer is to eliminate the craving itself.

At this point you may be asking yourself, "But isn't the whole premise of this book wanting and then getting something? Wanting and then learning how to gain satisfaction in our work?" Good point. And yes, it is. But the process here is different from the usual approach. Rather than making our way toward a predetermined goal (such as a better job or more money), we are instead uncovering or rediscovering our true and natural selves, determining what it is that truly makes us happy and then learning how to authentically express ourselves through our work. This second step simply helps us to discover what has prevented us from doing this all along. It may not be pretty to look at, but it is imperative that we take a look if we truly want a happy work life.

So know that you can do this and that you are worth the effort. Take the challenge of this step and your work life will no longer be dull, boring or hateful. And you will be a fully actualized, happy-with-your-work sentient being.

*He who boasts of his own ability*
*will not endure.*
*He who must always be right*
*has no distinction.*
*He who brings attention to himself*
*does not shine.*
*He who brags about himself*
*has no merit.*
*He who praises himself*
*cannot know who he really is.*

*If you want to know your truth,*
*just do your job, then let go.*
TAO TE CHING (#24)

# What We Don't Know Can Hurt Us

Too often we live in the future, especially when it comes to our jobs. We live for the weekend, we can't wait for vacations, we spend our raises before we get them, we look forward to the day we retire or get a promotion or move to another company. Approaching our jobs with our minds set in fantasy can only bring disappointment. This tendency to project ahead can be insidiously subtle. Sometimes we don't even know we're doing it; we only know that we're experiencing discomfort. This feeling that something isn't right can run from a mild, just-under-the-skin yearning to extreme anxiety attacks.

One way this tendency manifests itself is in the need-to-know syndrome. From the need to know what our boss is thinking to when our company might relocate, we believe that the only way to find relief is to learn all we can about whatever it is that haunts us. Often this need to know turns into a lament of "if only." We convince ourselves that if only we knew what was going on someplace else, we'd be happier and better able to do our job. Certainly ignorance of the truth can be a major cause of our pain. But sometimes we get so caught up in delusion that we cannot see the truth. What we think we need to know is usually none of our business.

Many of us have jobs that depend on others. (Before we look at what our ideal job might be, we must look at the job we have right now, so be patient.) And sometimes we do need to know when they will complete their task so that we can complete ours. So ask. Nothing wrong with that. It is when we don't get what we ask for or the answer we want that we stumble and fall off the track and set in motion the destructive cycle of obsession and blame that eventually affects our productivity and disposition. For instance, we might feel that if only we knew when the art department would finish the ad they're working on, then we could get on with what we're doing; or if only we knew how much money so-and-so was making, we'd know what kind of raise to ask for; or if only we knew what the company's relocation plans were, then we could get on with our job without worry—whatever it is, at least we'd know.

Anytime you ask and don't get the answer you want, your task is to cast away this desire to know and move on, rather than let this craving overtake you and send you into states you'd rather not be in. Move on to something else. Let go of the need to know. Sit in the not-knowing and trust that the truth will reveal itself in time. You will know what you need to know. In fact, you have all the information you need concerning the people and places around you at work. If you feel it isn't enough, then it's time to look at yourself. That's the hard part. But that's where true freedom from debilitating thirst comes from. Keep in mind that it is the inner clinging to the need to know rather than the not-knowing that entangles you.

Another way we project ourselves into the future is when we use the phrase "I can't wait." This is always followed by a time that hasn't yet come. I can't wait for the weekend, until tomorrow, till Christmas comes, till I can get some sleep, to watch TV tonight. On the surface none of this is bad—it's nice to gleefully anticipate pleasant things. But there's a big danger in wishing our lives away. Generally, this longing takes us out of the present and puts us in an unreal state, because we cannot know what the future will feel like. It takes us out of the present, which is where we are and the only place we can be. And if we base our idea of the future on our past experience, we might be robbing ourselves of some new sensations.

Begin to take notice of the language you use every day, particularly when speaking of the future. Take notice of how this language not only projects you ahead in your mind but also takes you away from what you're doing. Ask yourself why you want to be taken away. Ask yourself how good a job you can be doing if you're not completely present. Each time you hear yourself say something like "I can't wait," stop for a moment and look around you. Take notice of your immediate surroundings, of the colors of the walls, the tick of a clock, your coworker's plaid jacket. Center yourself with your breath, pay attention to the task in front of you and know that whatever you can't wait for will arrive in due time. And when you get there you will be there as fully as you are in this moment.

---

1. Write about how important time away from work is and how precious weekends and vacations are. How much time on the job do you spend thinking and dreaming about not being at work? Can you identify why this is?

2. Write about some of your recent or recurring need-to-know experiences and where they sent you.

3. Observe your language at and around work. Notice how often you use the phrase "if only." At

the end of each day review your interactions with the people you work with. Write about the issues and feelings that arise when you refrain from criticizing others and sit in a state of not knowing.

4. Notice how often at work you use a phrase such as "I can't wait." Each time you catch yourself, jot it down. Collect them all and write about them when you get home. Take note of the events or feelings that immediately preceded each wish to be someplace else. Can you identify a pattern? In using this phrase, in projecting into the future, what is it that you want to get away from? Write about this.

---

Joe worked for twenty years in a retail business. For most of that time he expressed disdain for his work and his employers. He was never happy and planned one day to quit and do something he loved. His true calling eluded him, but he was sure he'd figure it out if given the time. Meanwhile he complained about management (he could do a better job), other employees (he did a better job) and the customers (they were always wanting something and were never grateful). Joe was a smart and capable worker. Conscientious and hardworking, he gave much of himself to his job even though he would have preferred not to be there at all. In time Joe secured a middle management position that offered him some freedom to do things his way. But he had no respect for his boss, Pete, and their clashes affected everyone's morale.

All Joe could see was that his boss was an "idiot" and that if given the choice, employees would choose Joe as a boss rather than Pete. The tension in the store deepened when one employee was suspected of and then caught stealing significant sums of money. Apparently Pete was not closely involved with the day-to-day running of the store, so much of it fell to Joe. Joe got it from all sides. He felt he had to take action against the corrupt employee even though it wasn't really his job; he wanted to make changes in the way things were done and never got support from upper management; on top of it all he still hated his work. Joe had a bad back for years, which he blamed on the job. And now his mental and emotional health was being compromised. He suffered a nervous breakdown, though he never called it that, and took some time off from work just after the case against the corrupt employee exploded. After some time away Joe did not want to return to work, and didn't. But it devastated him to find out that the people at work didn't want him to return either.

Joe's answer was to move across the country with his family, far away from everything that reminded him of this experience. But financial pressures sent Joe looking for work before he had a chance to discover what he really wanted. So he ended up in the same business. But this time he got the top job in the store. Misery settled in quickly, though, as Joe found himself doing what he swore he'd never do again—proof that external changes do little to solve internal conflicts. After a year Joe quit his job to try once and for all to find the work that he loved. Joe swears he will never return to the same business, and we can all hope for his sake that he keeps his promise. But Joe has a lot of work to do on himself before he will know which path to pursue. It is clear that much of his dissatisfaction came from within and from the storm of confusion generated by "if only," the need to know, and "I can't wait." Joe lived in the possibility of quitting his job and in what was next for him. Because of this, he ruined his health and never even got close to an idea of his dream job. Again, it was his clinging to what wasn't real rather than the job itself that created so much havoc.

---

Do you identify with any of Joe's issues and struggles?

If so, what is your version of this story? Write about that.

If not, what do you feel about Joe and his experiences, about the decisions he made? Write about this.

---

During all those years perhaps Joe was afraid that if he looked inside to discover what his dream job was, he'd come up with nothing at all, so he decided not to look. This attitude will solve nothing and will only keep us stuck in delusional fantasy. The fastest and healthiest way to discover the truth about anything is to live in what is and stay away from the dangerous terrain of what isn't.

# Issues of Control and Power

As children, we learned to fear the mythical bogeyman. But time passes and we outgrow our childish fears. As adults, we give no thought to bogeymen, not realizing that we've co-opted them. Almost without our knowing it, they begin to appear in the form of pride, jealousy and anger. These bogeymen rob us of our natural inner peace and serenity.

Pride, jealousy, anger: the three bogeymen of serenity. They appear without warning wherever there's an imbalance of power, which means that in nearly every work situation these bogeymen are always on call, ready to pounce. There are employers (the ones with the power) and employees (those subject to the power). There are managers, bosses and supervisors—all with some degree of authority, power and control. And then there are the subordinates, workers and assistants—all subservient to the powers that be. But certainly our bosses have bosses, and even the top dog has to answer to someone, if only the shareholders. There are very few (I would argue none at all) who have absolute power, so the issue of power and control is relative and affects us all. But our apparent lack of power often incites the three bogeymen, and once they're in charge we become completely powerless. We give away our power as we convince ourselves that we are asserting it—a big-time delusion from which many of us suffer. Marie's story shows us how these three bogeymen, when they go on a rampage, can take us hostage and turn us into creatures that betray our true nature.

Marie is one of four executive assistants to the CEO of a major organization. She works directly for this CEO, but her work supervisor is one of the other three assistants. Marie loves her job. She has much autonomy, many fringe benefits and great respect and admiration for the CEO. But the way Marie feels about her supervisor, Diane, is another story. Marie's pride, jealousy and anger were recently activated and created such a raging emotional storm that Marie was ready to quit this job she so loves. You probably won't be surprised to hear that the trigger for this was a small and seemingly insignificant occurrence.

Marie's office is separated from Diane's by the CEO's sprawling office quarters, so throughout each day, unless they make a point of it, they rarely see each other. But Marie is self-motivating and doesn't need or want constant supervision, and according to her Diane isn't much of a manager anyway, so the physical arrangement suits them both. Marie's position affords her a look at nearly every piece of paper that floats in and out of the office— and there's a great deal of it. One bit of information she wishes had never come to her attention was the amount of Diane's previous year's bonus. Marie did not get a bonus, so the jealousy bogeyman took special note and tucked it away for future reference. Marie's position in the company did not qualify her for a bonus, but this fact did nothing to diminish her jealousy. Diane has been Marie's supervisor for nearly fifteen years, and Marie has never respected Diane's managerial style. So the bonus really stuck in her craw and fed her resentment.

Recently Marie and the other two assistants decided that they wanted to attend a benefit concert that the CEO was sponsoring. Marie called the cosponsor to ask for three tickets. They were often given tickets to events, one of the perks of the job, but this event was unique and so they had to make a special request. Marie decided not to ask Diane if she would like to go, justifying it with the thought that Diane never attends such events anyway, so there was no need to ask.

There were a few things going on here that Marie didn't see until much later, after it all blew up. Marie's jealousy, pride and anger were at work convincing her that she needn't ask Diane or even tell her about it. Marie wanted to go, period. She thought that if she asked her about it, Diane would not want to go herself and would tell Marie that she and the other women shouldn't go either, that it was inappropriate to ask for free tickets. Since Marie wanted to go, her desire set the following in motion.

She made the call. She got the tickets. No problem. The cosponsor asked if there was anyone else who wanted a ticket. Marie said no, at that moment not heeding the inner voice that said maybe she should ask Diane. The next day the cosponsor phoned Diane, told her of Marie's call and asked if she'd like a ticket. It turned out that Diane did want to go. She later let it be known to one of the other assistants that she was completely embarrassed by that phone call and that Marie had undermined her authority by asking for the tickets, which caused her great upset.

Marie heard of this on Friday and spent the weekend sorting through it all. At first she was stubbornly defiant. Her anger blurred her vision. She could see nothing clearly. In her mind she had done nothing wrong, a statement that became a mantra as she struggled toward peace of mind. She did not want to face Diane's wrath (notwithstanding the fact that in all the years she had known her, Diane had never exhibited wrath). Her pride kicked in, and she decided that she couldn't and wouldn't apologize. Then the jealousy spread—the money Diane made, the position she had—and Marie was ready to quit her job. Marie ranted and raved for a while, getting it all out, spilling her guts to friends. She did not want to go back to the office on Monday.

At the end of the weekend, having talked about it, written about it, prayed about it and taken advice about it, Marie was ready to hear her own truth. She was ready to be responsible and face up to what she had to do. Once her anger died down she was able to see how defiant she could be. In not asking Diane, even after her inner voice told her to, she saw how her anger and jealousy controlled her. She hadn't asked Diane because she didn't want to give Diane the opportunity to exert her power over Marie and deny her a ticket. So rather quickly she was able to see that she owed Diane an apology for not asking her in the first place. However, her angry defiance was still engaged as she said: "But I'll be damned if I'm going to apologize and then stand there and be subjected to her scolding as she tells me how embarrassed she was and what a naughty girl I was. I just can't do that. I'll apologize and then leave. That much I can do."

What it took Marie another two days to see was the real issue underlying it all: the question of who is in charge. Because of her autonomy, her relationship with the CEO and her lack of respect for Diane's management skills, Marie forgot that, whether she likes it or not, Diane is her boss. It is not up to Marie how the department is run. It is up to Diane. And Marie finally realized that what she had to apologize for was going over Diane's head and making the phone call requesting the tickets before consulting with her. The issue was not about whether or not Diane wanted to go. Once Marie saw the real issue and accepted her responsibility, she felt much better. She was able to accept the fact— because it is indeed a fact—that Diane is her boss and she must answer to her whether she agrees with Diane's style or not. It is not her job to decide how the office is run. It is her job to do her job and to respect the flow of authority.

So Marie apologized to Diane without carrying in any bogeymen. She was humble and sincere. Diane, of course, was grateful for Marie's honesty and did not berate her and go on about her own embarrassment. She was gracious. They both were. Marie didn't quit her job; she still loves it and has adopted a completely new and different attitude toward Diane and her shortcomings as a boss. Somehow they are not so important anymore.

And after working together for so many years, Diane and Marie are beginning to change their relationship as a direct result of this incident. A few weeks after Marie cleared the air with Diane, Diane apologized to Marie for something completely unrelated to the above incident. According to Marie, this is a "never-before occurrence, which I think illustrates the powerful changes that occur when we (with the help of friends) venture out of our comfort zone." Surprising things happen when we're open and honest with ourselves and others.

---

1. How do the three bogeymen—pride, anger and jealousy—figure into your daily work life? Write about this.

2. Is there some incident with your boss that you have not forgotten and are still stubbornly holding on to? Can you just for a moment forget your boss's actions and focus exclusively on your own? How did you behave? How would you have liked to behave? Write about this. What conclusions can you draw after looking objectively at the situation? Write them down. And if you are ready, take the actions you feel would bring some peace of mind.

3. How many times a day, a week, do you say to yourself or someone else: "I can't stand my job, and I wish I could quit"? For one week just pay

attention and notice if this comment follows any particular activity or situation. Note the connections, if any.

4. Then, the next week, each time this thought arises, replace it with its opposite: "I love my job, and I'm glad to have it." Even if you don't quite mean it, express this gratitude. See if anything at all shifts. Write about the week as it goes along.

---

# Frustrated Ambitions

Perhaps the most crucial impediment that we need to cast away as we progress toward the realization of our true work and enjoyment of it is our dualistic thinking. This operates everywhere and becomes especially vivid when we consider our status in the workplace.

When we are young we may or may not know what we want to do when we grow up, but we are certainly encouraged to think about it. And usually our visions of the future are quite grand whenever we playact our dreams. This fantasizing isn't in itself a bad thing, but sometimes when we are middle-aged we ask ourselves, "What happened?" We sense dissatisfaction; we look around and cannot help but compare our place in life with that of others (especially as it relates to work). And because of the nature of organizations and their inherent hierarchy, most of us feel disappointment, particularly if we are or once were ambitious. There is always someone doing better, there is always someone higher, happier, healthier.

However we describe what we see, if we are unhappy, our situation is bad and any other situation is good. We decide that we have failed and wonder where we went wrong. On top of this we are bombarded daily by media images of successful people. We look toward celebrities to assist us in making life choices, and then when we look back at ourselves we can't help but be disappointed.

We may be doing exactly what we were meant to do, exactly what we've always wanted to do, but we end up not enjoying it because it just isn't enough.

Betty is at a point in her life where all she can see is failure, even if that isn't the truth. As she approaches two very significant anniversaries, Betty finds herself reflecting on three important questions of life: "Who am I? Where am I from? Where am I going?" Anniversaries and birthdays mark the passage of time and are potent opportunities for us to reflect on the impermanent nature of life. Some of us shy away from celebrating these events either because we usually end up disappointed (that is, we set up high expectations and never get what we want) or because we would rather not face the natural process of aging. But whether we acknowledge them or not, these markers are there, beating time, so better to celebrate them than deny them. Betty will soon mark sixteen years of freedom from a serious addiction to drugs and alcohol and next year will turn fifty years old. But Betty is not in a mood to celebrate, stuck as she is in self-doubt, loathing and fear.

First, let's take an objective look at Betty's life. A talented writer, performer and comedienne, Betty has for most of her adult life worked in the creative world of theater. It is her passion. Some of the highlights of her past: she designed and crafted lifelike doll-puppets that were displayed and sold in several Manhattan stores; she toured and performed for many years with a prominent children's theater company; she wrote, produced and performed several of her one-woman shows in New York City and Boston. Today Betty is a core member of a small ensemble theater group in Manhattan that each week performs its own original material. Some members of the company have moved on and are enjoying successful careers on network television. Recently Betty produced and starred in two of her own one-act plays, and she has since expanded one of them and will stage it again soon. This play has caught the interest of a literary agent, and Betty is working on a proposal to turn it into a book. Betty owns an apartment in New York and is president of her co-op board. She has also successfully conquered her addiction to drugs and alcohol, one day at a time, and will soon have under her belt as many years sober as she spent drunk—an impressive accomplishment given how powerful the demon of drink can be.

Next, let's look at how Betty sees her life. Right now she is focused on all the missed opportunities and the fact that no one is calling her to star in her own sitcom. She judges her life a failure, especially when her envy of her theater companions is engaged. Rather than being happy for their success, all she can say is, "What about me?" Though there isn't a plethora of acting opportunities for women her age, she blames herself for not working more and making lots of money in her chosen profession. When she looks back on her life she regrets much of it. Sometimes the fear from her active addiction years creeps forward and clouds her present-day judgment and sense of herself. Hence, self-loathing is a current theme that runs through her daily life and sinks her into a depression.

Seven years ago Betty was at another low point in her life and decided that theater (an unpredictable and often low-paying existence) was keeping her on the fringes of society. So she decided to jump into the mainstream and work a nine-to-five job that would give her a regular paycheck, health insurance, and a "real" job that her family could relate to. She got a job that didn't exactly suit her and then for years worked very hard trying to fit herself into it. But rather than seeing it as a poor fit, she blamed first herself for her predicament and then the corporation for not discovering her brilliance. In fact, Betty worked in a dysfunctional department that was all but neglected by upper management, as their long-term plans were to phase it out. Betty did not know this, so her self-esteem slowly eroded. During this time Betty continued as a vibrant member of her theater group and produced some of her best work to date. But she was miserable each day from nine to five, and the suffering carried over into the rest of her life.

After much writing, talking and meditating on her circumstances, Betty finally mustered up the courage to quit her job—but not before a last-ditch effort to land another position in the industry that she thought might be more suited to her talents, and not before the toll on her self-esteem was grave. Three weeks after Betty quit, her department was phased out and the other members of the department were offered a severance package. Betty blames herself for not staying longer to benefit from this compensation, but she had no crystal ball and her bottom-line-oriented company wasn't about to offer her this information. So even here, with something that she had absolutely no control over, Betty views herself as having failed.

What Betty can't see right now because she is stuck in the cycle of thwarted ambition and self-hatred is that her attachment to status (having a "real" job, being a sitcom star or well-known and well-paid working actress) has blinded her to the truth of who she is, where she's come from and where she's going. The reality is that Betty has spent all of her life involved in work that satisfies her and gives her life meaning. She has an innate talent for writing and performing (something she doesn't deny), but she takes it for granted. The hungry ghost in Betty is simply never satisfied. We all have this insatiable desire working in us to some degree and at various times throughout our life. And perhaps people like Betty suffer more acutely from it because of their actively imaginative minds. But no matter what, the two warring sides—the blessing and the curse, the good and the bad, right and wrong—need to be reconciled, for as long as we continue to see the world in dualistic terms we will continue to suffer. So casting away the dualistic labels and seeing things as they are is not only Betty's challenge right now but yours as well. If you truly want to love what you do with your life, you must cast aside your frustrated ambitions, ignore your bruised ego and not feed your status-hungry demons.

---

1. If you don't already love the business you're in and the daily work you do, pretend for a moment that you do. With that a given, are you happy with your status in the company? Is there another position you'd prefer? Is it about the work itself, the money attached to it or the status of it? Write about this.

2. Do you know what field you would love to be working in? Are you in it today? Why not? Did you pursue a career due to family or societal pressure? Did you fall into a job, get lazy and attached to the ease of it or to the financial rewards of it and decide to stay put despite the dissatisfaction quotient? Write about whatever reveries these questions spark. And be honest.

3. Write about any and all missed opportunities, perceived and real, involving work. Describe how your life might be different if you had followed a different path. Who or what got in your way of realizing your dreams? Are you still blaming and holding on to old resentments? Be honest; don't spare anyone here, including yourself. You are just

gathering the seeds of your discontent in one place so that you can look squarely and clearly into your past and finally deal with it in order to live comfortably and happily in the present.

4. If you're in the field of your dreams and still dissatisfied, write about why you think that is. What is blocking your gratitude and true enjoyment of your work?

5. How does your dualistic way of thinking affect your outlook on your chosen career? On your present circumstances? On your vision of yourself? Write about this.

---

## Work Can Be a Drug (an Escape, an Excuse, a Reason, an Alibi)

Sometimes we simply do not want to face ourselves. There is nothing wrong with taking a break from self-examination once in a while, but often this break becomes a way of life and we never return to the mirror because our mind tells us that it will be just too painful. We are afraid of what we might find. Meanwhile we sit in the pain caused by our refusal to look, and all we can do is learn to live with it.

One of the ways we avoid looking at our life is by burying ourselves completely in our work. We live, sleep and eat work. We never stop thinking about it even when we find ourselves doing something else. Work defines us, shapes us, controls us. We call it passion, and others believe and even envy us. But often it is addiction. There is nothing wrong with being passionate about work, but when it begins to affect your health or when your life becomes unmanageable as a result or when nothing else matters, then you can be sure you've slipped over the line into obsessive-compulsive behavior. If you want some measure of balance in your life and some spiritual peace of mind, it is imperative that you take stock and begin to change your approach to work.

Denial is the glue that reinforces a work addict's fortress. And though on the surface it might appear that a work addict is suffering from the thirst for more, it is quite the opposite. What they suffer from is a thirst for nonexistence. They use work to lose themselves, to run away from life, to avoid looking inside themselves. This is a tendency we all have to some extent, and it gets manifested in myriad ways. But because of the nature of work, the demands it places on us, the fact that most of us work and understand the inherent pressures, it is easy for someone to get lost in the drug of work without anyone noticing, least of all the addict.

Noreen is a vice president of a large service-oriented corporation. It is a prestigious, demanding and well-compensated position that Noreen's years of experience qualify her for. Noreen has worked hard to get where she is and deserves to be there. But fear rules Noreen's life, causing her to hold on so tightly that breathing deeply is sometimes a problem. And though she clings to her job as if it were a life raft, in reality it is a noose that keeps getting tighter and tighter. Because of the denial factor, Noreen would not even recognize herself in this description. But the truth is that she spends way more time on the job than is necessary, and she invests so much of herself in the problems of her job that it affects her emotional, physical and spiritual health. She doesn't take time from the exhausting demands of work until her body breaks down and she's forced to remain in bed. Otherwise she would feel as though she were cheating. Even though intellectually she knows she's capable, someplace inside she believes she'll be found out and dismissed. Having once been out of work for more than a year feeds this fear and fuels her maniacal devotion. Perhaps she subconsciously believes that if she is away from work too long, her coworkers will determine that they can get along without her.

Gayle, another woman in a high-stakes vice presidential position for a large corporation, is quite like Noreen. They could almost be the same woman: both addicted to work, both in denial about it, both so intensely energetic toward their work that no one would dare question their claim to love what they do. Outwardly, though, they couldn't be more different. Noreen, brooding and serious, often looks as though she has the weight of the world on her shoulders. Gayle is always smiling and appears as if she hasn't a care in the world. But looks can be deceiving. For both women, work is a balm that helps them cope with the issues and situations in their personal lives. But they also use it to run away from their problems. The surface of each life has a different texture, but the underlying themes are identical. Noreen appears to work on her personal life as hard as she works on the job, using therapy and support groups to understand her pain. Gayle agreed to let her ex-husband be the main caregiver for their child and sometimes uses the excuse of work to shorten or delay her time with her child. If their jobs were taken from them, both women would be disoriented and confused. Despite their claims to love their work, it's likely that neither has given much thought to what her ideal job would be. If given the choice to do anything at all, they'd probably stay put for fear of admitting that their lives up to then had been lies. And the fear of being unmoored is too great to take the risk.

While most of us are probably not addicted to work, many of us use work as a handy excuse to rationalize our spiritual lethargy: "I'm too tired at the end of the day to even think about meditating" or "There isn't enough time in my day to eat properly, let alone write about my work life." Work can also be a convenient scapegoat for avoiding other parts of our lives. "I'm too busy to see you tonight or to take a vacation," for instance. It also supports us as we explain our ill manners and rude behavior: "Sorry I'm late, I got caught up at work." And too often we blame work for our bad moods, taking no responsibility for our disposition. But the fact that we have to work for a living doesn't mean we can't love our work and is certainly no reason to blame it for our unhappiness.

---

1. Do you know someone who appears to work longer and harder than you do? How does this make you feel about them? About you? Or do you work longer and harder than everyone else does? Why?
2. How honest are you with yourself and others?

   - Do you ever beg out of social events using work as the reason? How often is it true?
   - Do you ever blame your cranky disposition on something that happened at work, mistreating those you love?
   - Do you ever work later than necessary to avoid facing a difficulty at home?
   - Do you ever hide out at work?
   - Do you ever procrastinate on tasks at work, so when you finally get to them and finish them you've made yourself late for dinner again?

3. Do you feel there is a good balance in your life between the personal and the professional? If not, describe what you would like to change, how you would like it to be. What's interfering with this becoming a reality?

4. Do you spend time each day on spiritual matters? Or do you find excuses and never seem to have the time? Can you for one week schedule fifteen minutes a day to sit quietly alone? Do this and notice the changes in your work attitude. Write about it.

---

There are times when work will take us away from another commitment and create disappointment. This is unavoidable and excusable. But when we use work to shield us from other aspects of our lives that we're just not up to facing, eventually we will pay a price. We will begin to believe ourselves and blame work for our inadequacies, which in turn will create animosity toward work when it isn't the real culprit. No relationship can withstand such abuse. It is up to us then to be open, honest and fair about our part in this relationship. And when we start treating our work relationship with care, then we will be clear about where the abuse, if any, is coming from. (Some work situations are abusive, but we cannot be clear about this until we clean up our own behavior. And once we do, the clarity that comes will make our choices evident and easy.) So if you take the time to listen carefully to yourself and the words and phrases you use to describe your relationship with work and how it affects the rest of your life, you will mitigate your discomfort. And the negative feelings you have toward your work will gradually slip away.

# Money — There's Nothing Wrong with It

Money. Can't live with it. Can't live without it. Surely we all know what the can't-live-without-it part means. We need money to survive, to house, feed and clothe ourselves and our families. We also need it to supplement the basics and add more comfort and pleasure to our daily lives. Nothing wrong with this. This is not a bad thing. Yet when this need turns into an insatiable craving, we move into the can't-live-with-it side of the picture, and no matter how much money we have, it isn't enough. Then the destructive cycle of greed, anger and folly is engaged, and money becomes our god, our obsession, our sole goal. We grasp for it, we hoard it, we spend it carelessly or we even turn our backs on it, all in a mad, vain attempt to secure our happiness. The truth in the saying "Money is the root of all evil" certainly stems from this reckless and selfish abandon that we employ in the race to the procurement of or freedom from money.

Whenever we do anything solely for the money, the price we end up paying is worth more than whatever money we make. As you will come to see (or as you may already know from experience), when our work becomes an activity that is just about getting paid, then the work loses meaning and we are no longer gratified—even the money, the reason we took on the work in the first place, doesn't satisfy. Similarly, when we are given large sums of money for nothing, we also pay a great toll. It loses its value, and we lose our respect for it and for ourselves in the process.

Evelyn was born into a family of great wealth. When she left the family home to be on her own, she never had to worry about money. Each month she was given a hefty income, and if she ever needed or wanted more, it was there. While this arrangement seems ideal and greatly appeals to those of us who have always had to work for a living, it can have its own burdens. And for many years it was an albatross weighing down Evelyn's self-worth. She became a dilettante, dabbling in many different arenas and settling in none. This is not necessarily a waste of time, but in Evelyn's case the satisfaction of a job well done rarely came. She got paid for most of her work, yet she was never highly motivated, and a deep inner sense of failure plagued her. For a few years Evelyn even decided to support herself exclusively with the money she made. She didn't give back her family's money; she simply let it sit in the bank. But because Evelyn never gave herself to her work (it was always about the money), she eventually got tired of what she was doing and moved on. Compelled to dip back into her trust fund, she nursed a huge resentment toward her family and the money. She believed that if the money hadn't been there, she would have been forced to do something with her life. She felt she was spinning her wheels, neither moving along nor stopping anywhere long enough to gain some self-respect.

When it was suggested to Evelyn that she could easily relieve her money misery by giving it all away, she was taken aback. This solution had never occurred to her, but upon hearing it from someone else, she was instantly awakened to the folly of her ways. Never before had she entertained the real possibility of actually not having this money. She took it for granted and knew it would always be there for her and her children (when she had them) and their children and on and on. When Evelyn thought through the idea of emptying her bank accounts, she confronted her own greed and lack of gratitude. After so many years of self-hatred she saw how the money had nothing to do with the way she felt about herself, and she knew that even without the money this attitude wouldn't change. It was then that she decided to make her pursuit of work not be about money. She also realized that the money she had needn't be such a burden. Understanding what a gift it really was, she resolved to use it to fulfill her wish to be useful in the world.

So Evelyn went back to school and is now happily involved in a private therapeutic practice. Her own personal struggles help her to be a truly empathic healer. She continues, of course, to deal with the curve balls that life throws at her, but the issue of money vis-à-vis work has ceased to be a disruptive force. Today Evelyn appreciates more than ever the gifts in her life, including the inherited money. She no longer takes these gifts for granted, particularly since the arrival of her two beautiful children. The work of being a good parent and helping others outside the family has completely satisfied her inner yearning for meaning. The daily tasks of caring for her family and nurturing her nascent practice supply her with all the meaning she needs. Her work is her spiritual practice, and her spiritual practice is her work.

"Yeah, but if I had her money, my life would be so much easier, and I'd be able to do just exactly what I want to do without worrying about paying the bills." If you think this or if you've ever dreamt of winning the lottery, sure that either would ease your worries, it's time to think again and look at why your mind goes there in the first place. It is not money or winning the lottery but the desperate desire for them that creates our unhappiness. And the idea that money is the root of all evil doesn't mean that when we have money like Evelyn's or when we win the lottery we will become mean and evil and behave badly. What it means is that when we begin to crave such riches, we commit acts that betray our good and true nature. We let the deep-seated and gut-wrenching desire for money compromise our own moral values. While this may seem overstated and exaggerated, how many of us have sold out for money? At first it may seem a small thing and not so devastating, but time takes its toll, and eventually we become a shell of our true selves as we justify our behavior and let fear guide us.

A city newspaper was recently barraged with lawsuits when it misprinted the winning numbers for a lottery-style game that it runs. Thousands of people thought they had won large sums of money. When told that they hadn't, they got angry and hired lawyers. They lost nothing but their fantasy, a moment's dream of riches. They were disappointed. They felt cheated. Someone had to take responsibility for that, though certainly not them. So they sued because they couldn't let go of the idea of getting something for nothing and figured a lawsuit might give them even more easy money. For our purposes the lottery is simply a convenient metaphor for any money fixation. It could be wanting a promotion at work simply for the bigger paycheck, longing for a job that would support a lifestyle you're sure you'd be happier in or banking all your extra money today (and denying yourself some pleasure now) so that you can retire early and finally enjoy your life. What all of these aspirations have in common is an extreme desire for money or for those things that money can buy. This yearning only serves to take us away from our real life *now* and project us into the unreal future. It not only prevents us from enjoying any task but undermines our gratitude for what we have now and sows bitterness and discontentment, so that even if we are working in the field of our dreams, we cannot enjoy it to the fullest, and our contribution is definitely not at 100 percent. Whenever we make money all-important and allow it to distract us from the task at hand, it is possible we will never do the work we love.

This does not mean that we should work for nothing. But when money is our first and only priority, then we are surely destined to be unhappy at work. Unlike

Evelyn, most of us were not born into money and do have to work for a living. But why does this simple reality so often turn into a tired and knee-jerk resentment? We sometimes claim to be a victim of necessity without realizing that we are our own captors. Rather than focusing on what you don't have (the dream job, lots of money), look at what you do have. Appreciate the fact that you're able to work at all. Challenge yourself every day to find something in your work to be grateful for. And then decide to enjoy each task as you confront it. Once you begin to like what you do, then you will be ready to do what you love.

Having money is not so terrible. In fact, it is necessary for getting along in the world and can even provide us with the means to practice charity. What is terrible is the selfish desire for money and what this desire makes us do. It may take some time to understand the distinction, but know that having money or not having money is not where your problems with money lie. It is in the craving for money or the yearning to be relieved of money troubles that we lose our perspective and let money rule our lives. So your job here is to cast away your desire for money. Then you can do your work mindfully and contentedly. And when you do, the money will come. Concentrate on the letting go. Come back again and again to this notion as you come back to your breath when sitting still. The rewards will be yours when you loosen your grip on them. This works, it truly works.

1. How preoccupied are you with money? How does it figure into your enjoyment of or your dissatisfaction with work? Write about this.

2. Does fear of losing what you have or not getting what you want or think you deserve influence your attitude and approach toward work? Does this motivate or stifle you? Why? Write about this.

3. Write about money—what it means to you, what your parents' values about money were, how much you make, how much you want to make, how your identity is tied into how much you make. Does money make you happy, sad, angry? Does a lack of money affect your self-esteem? This might prove to be the most difficult exercise in this book. Writing about and being honest about how we deal with, feel about and think of money can be as sensitive as writing about sex. It's very personal, it's very intimate. And we don't usually talk directly about it, we talk around it. So it may take a few tries here to get honest, but keep at it. This is important.

4. Have you ever sold out for money? Describe the circumstances. What did you gain? What did you lose? Without slipping into remorse, write about what you could have done differently. What have you learned?

5. With your opposite hand (the one you don't normally write with) spend ten minutes writing a

gratitude list. (This is an extremely important exercise, as it will not only focus you completely on the task of writing this list, engaging the half of your brain that is underused and giving you a sense of what total concentration feels like, but also bring your attention to what is most important in your life.)

6. How important is money here? Did you have fun writing this list? Did it give you a new perspective on what you have in your life? Write about this.

7. Write a gratitude list with your usual hand. How does this list, and the experience of writing it, differ from exercise 5?

8. Repeat exercise 5 any time money and the pursuit of it dominates your thoughts, any time the desire for more or the fear of loss preoccupies you, and each time you want a new perspective on something. Consider writing this list for five minutes at the end of each day to take stock in the gifts you have.

---

## Using Envy to Reach Your Goals

Okay, so you want things. There's no getting around it and no easy way to discard these desires. It's time to really look at what you want and why. Often our desire is stimulated when we see what others have. Our envy button gets pushed as advertisers and entertainment companies spend lots of money to stir up our insatiable greed. This all relates to work because work is usually our source of income, and if the money we make isn't able to satisfy all our desires, then we become angry and disillusioned with our jobs and then unhappy both at work and at home.

So let's indulge ourselves here and spend some time enumerating our petty desires along with our deepest ones.

---

1. Write a random and comprehensive list of all the tangible things you would like to have that you don't now have (in no particular order).
2. Now prioritize the list by placing numbers before each item, with the number 1 being assigned to the most desired thing.
3. Then for the top ten items on the list assign a number from 1 to 5 that indicates the intensity of your desire, with 1 being low and 5 being high.
4. For each of these ten items write a paragraph or two about how having them would change or not change your life and how not having them now affects your life.
5. Repeat exercises 1 to 4 with a list of intangible things you would like to have in your life. (This could include relationships, feelings, states of mind.)
6. Repeat exercises 1 to 4 with work-related desires (perhaps your ideal job, a new boss, a different schedule).

7. On a separate piece of paper write down the most-desired thing from each list and put it aside for the moment. Then collect all the pages you've written on to complete the exercises in this section and make a ritual of burning or otherwise destroying them. Choose a time when you can be alone. Read over (preferably out loud) what you've written and sit quietly, absorbing the extent of your own desires and the dissatisfaction they've created. Then shred the papers into tiny pieces and/or safely burn them. As you watch them disappear, imagine your desire for them also going up in smoke. Be willing—even just for the time it takes to do this exercise—to let them go.

8. Afterward sit quietly again and absorb the impact of this ritual. Write about the feelings it evoked and what effect, if any, it had on your wish list.

9. Now look at the three desires you wrote down and set aside. Is your level of desire for these things the same as it was when you first wrote about them? Concentrate on the work-related desire and write about what you could do to attain it. And if it still feels that your life would be more complete with it than without it, then make a plan that will move you toward getting it. And decide, since it is so important to have this thing, that everything along the way you must do to get it will be as important, as valued and as pleasing as the thing itself. Each act, each chore is a part of the thing

itself because without them you cannot have it. If you see each of these things in this way, then you will see that in the doing of these things you already have them. Absorb yourself in these details, enjoy the process of getting to it, and maybe when you get there it will feel as though you've had it all along.

---

# There Are No Coincidences

For a moment let's look at the natural law of cause and effect and its impact on our everyday lives. For every action there is a reaction. Anytime we take an action (cause) something happens (effect). This is not a difficult principle to grasp. But sometimes we get so focused on what we want to happen or expect to happen that we miss the real effect altogether. Or worse, we do not take responsibility for the effect because it differs from the way we envisioned it, or it occurs so long after the fact that we refuse to see a causal connection.

As we have learned, desire is the first cause of disillusionment and disappointment. This unquenchable thirst causes us to exert our will to get what we want, but this exertion of will always has consequences—consequences that we are responsible for. These fruits of our actions are, relatively, either good or bad. A good action produces a good effect; a bad action, a bad effect. This has nothing to do with moral judgment or reward and punishment. It is simply a straightforward manifestation of the law of cause and effect. And sometimes the results can be life-altering.

A series of volitional actions (cause) cost Tricia her job (effect). (We will not define any of what transpired here as good or bad, as everything is relative, and perhaps Tricia's job loss will in the end be a good thing for her.) Tricia worked as a manager for a large hotel chain, overseeing the housekeeping staff, which was part of a large union. Because of the service nature of the business and its close contact with the public, there were many rules and regulations that the staff was required to follow. And it was incumbent upon the managers to enforce these rules. One such regulation was that female room attendants wear panty hose under their uniforms. Tricia suspected a room attendant of flouting this requirement (she had just asked her to remove some jewelry that was also against regulations) because when she was asked to change, it took less time than Tricia thought it should. So Tricia lifted up the room attendant's dress to see for herself. This volitional action had consequences that only Tricia is responsible for. It is irrelevant here whether the room attendant was abiding by the rules or not. What is relevant is that when Tricia lifted up the uniform (her volitional action) she should have known that she was flagrantly abusing the strict codes that regulated her own behavior as a manager.

The union got involved, of course, and management was called in. Tricia was given an opportunity to apologize for her behavior in a small forum. But she was willfully defensive, and her apology was clearly insincere. The apology wasn't accepted, things escalated and Tricia was given another chance to make amends to a larger group, but her stubborn pride kept her from it. Management was then forced to terminate Tricia, who sees herself as a victim and self-righteously points to the room attendant for causing the problem. What she can't see yet is the clear cause-and-effect scenario, stuck as she is in the haze of self-justification. But her actions (cause) were clearly responsible for getting her fired (effect).

Tricia will either slip even deeper into bitterness and resentment (which will affect her future employment possibilities) or use this experience as a stepping-stone to personal awareness and growth. She may decide that managing others is not her forte, or she will learn how to be a more compassionate and fair manager in the future. Whatever she decides, in order to be happy in her work life she must first take full responsibility for her part in the drama.

---

1. Do you take responsibility for all your volitional actions? Or do you see yourself as a victim when something goes wrong and as a hero when things go right?
2. Describe an incident at work that you feel went badly. Go back to the beginning and objectively

look at your behavior all along the way. Where did you try to exert your will? Were you able to detach and let things take their natural course, or did you attempt to interfere and try to control the outcome?

3. Now describe an incident that ended up going well. Ask the same questions as above.

4. In both cases can you see the principle of cause and effect operating, whether the result was good or bad? Write about this.

---

A normal response to accepting the truth that good actions create good effects and bad actions bad effects is to decide to engage only in good actions. But this stance can get us into trouble. The good results can stimulate our craving for more good results, which will send us off into the world of desire that is never satisfied. So perhaps it's time to look at the alternative. First we must come to an understanding that any volitional action, good or bad, simply keeps us caught in the cycle of desire and attachment. When we realize this we can move toward simply accepting things as they are. Sometimes things happen. Sometimes no one is responsible. It is just how it is, the way things go, life on life's terms. This doesn't mean that we should sit back and do nothing. For it is only when we take volitional actions—or those driven by self-will—that we get into trouble and cause ourselves pain. Actions taken with a pure heart and not attached to self-aggrandizement are simply actions taken. They are not subject to the usual consequences. Rarely do we suffer from the effects of such actions. We simply take in stride whatever the outcome is.

When we refrain from self-destructive volitional actions, we do the best we can and accept what comes. We detach ourselves from the wheel of desire and let ourselves just *be*. Only then do we experience peace and harmony no matter what happens around us.

## Wanting What We Want When We Want It

In this section we have seen how desire can cause so much pain. One of the reasons for this is because when we crave something that we do not yet have, we project ourselves into a future state, imagining what it would be like to have this object of our desire. And with this comes the desire to have it right now, to satisfy our longing now, not later. We take ourselves out of the present—the only reality there is—and spend time in our minds in the fantastical, not-yet-realized future. And when it hits us that our desires are simply unrealized, ephemeral dreams, we ache with pain. The only way out of this morass is to let go of these desires and live fully in the present.

If you've done the exercises in this section and taken this second step, you have uncovered and learned a great deal about yourself that will move you into freedom from desire and toward the ultimate freedom of loving what you do.

1. You looked at your behavior at work and how much of your mood is determined by what has not yet happened, by your need to know, and by your desire to be somewhere other than exactly where you are.

2. You became aware of how pride, jealousy and anger can undermine not only your performance at work but your daily enjoyment of the work itself.

3. You learned how your dualistic thinking can keep you away from the truth of yourself and your situation and can cause deep dissatisfaction in everything that you do.

4. You looked at how attached you are to your work—how it defines you, how you use it and it uses you—and how balanced your life is or isn't.

5. You came to an understanding of how money figures in the whole scheme of things and how driven you are by it.

6. You closely analyzed your deepest desires and took some concrete steps toward casting away envy and realizing your most important work desire.

7. You saw how the natural law of cause and effect operates, and you began to take some responsibility for the conditions of your life. Here you had a taste of just taking action and letting go of results.

In this second step you have seen how your troubles, large and small, arise out of your desire for and attachment to so many things, including money, power, ambition, control, ideas, opinions and beliefs. And you have been introduced to the notion that the only way you can transcend your craving and suffering is first to gain some understanding of it and then to just let it go. It is a process, and each day, if you are open to the challenge and willing to take risks, you get a little closer to who you are meant to be and what you are supposed to be doing. And with each day also comes a deeper and fuller appreciation of the work that you are doing right now.

> *Fill your cup to the brim*
> *and it will spill.*
> *Keep sharpening your blade*
> *and its edge will dull.*
> *Chase after money and security*
> *and you'll never be at peace.*
> *Let success breed arrogance*
> *and all manner of grief will assail you.*
>
> *Once your work is done, step back from it.*
> *This is the way to serenity.*
> TAO TE CHING (#9)

## The Third Step
# REALIZING THIS IS IT!

■

Once we understand the source of our dissatisfaction (the first step) we can then see deeper into our unquench-able thirst and move toward casting away these desires (the second step). After this uprooting of our delusions—that which causes us so much pain—we become ready to relax into our lives, to accept things as they are and to realize that there is an end to it all. Freedom exists. Joy, happiness and contentment with our work can be ours, in fact, are ours, right here, right now. We needn't wait for the perfect job to come along before we can be happy. We realize that by wishing for something differ-ent from what is, we are not only wishing our life away, we are never fully in it to begin with. So we must switch our perspective around and face whatever the present moment offers—not the past, not the future, but the present. And when we do, we realize that we have everything we need and want right now. Our life is com-plete, rich and full *as it is*. The task in front of us not only is worth doing, but fills us with gratitude. So we do it, get through it and move on naturally and smoothly to the next task—and so on and so on, until we are so completely absorbed in our work that there is no room for disillusionment or dissatisfaction.

And when we realize the truth that *this is it*, we live in harmony with whatever life throws at us, without being thrown by it. Equanimity and peace of mind become our natural states. When we recall our past disturbances we are simply amused by them—they no longer haunt us. And we give no mind to the future except as it becomes necessary to make plans.

Sound too good to be true? Well, it's not. It is possible for each one of us to live such an existence. All we really need to do is make the decision and then realize that by letting go of our desires we can attain freedom, which translates into a life of peace and contentment.

But we need to be willing to change and to entertain the idea that change is possible. This is not so hard when we realize that our old approach, our old way of doing things, simply doesn't work anymore—if indeed it ever did. Whatever it takes, we are ready.

Now, all of this does not mean that we must stay put and endure our work even if it is not our dream job. But we must employ some PEP. This is a favorite acronym of one of my teachers. It stands for *perseverance, endurance, patience*. It is often necessary to practice patience in our quest for the ideal work situation and trust that with the readiness of time (another expression of this same teacher) all will be revealed and we will realize our true calling.

Often we are exactly where we are meant to be, working in our field of choice in a position that is perfectly suited to us. But just as often, because of our nature to never be satisfied and our tendency to long for something other than what we have, we don't see this, focused as we are on the past or the future. So our work in this step is to turn our gaze toward whatever is happening at *this* moment, not on what has already happened or on what might happen next.

It sounds so easy. But the challenge is a big one. The rewards, though, are even greater and more potent than you could ever imagine. Even so, even with such a promise, it is not easy to incorporate this step into your daily life. Your busy mind (and schedule) and your hopes, fears and anxieties will continue to plague you and keep you off course. But there is a path to follow that will lead you to the realization of your truth. And steps four to seven will elucidate this path. So here in step three you will simply work on realizing the truth that there is an end to your dissatisfaction and that this end is in the here and now. You will work toward realizing that when you let go of your cravings you attain not only freedom but also daily peace and contentment.

*Fame or happiness, which is more cherished?*
*Money or health, which is more valuable?*
*Gain or loss, which is more beneficial?*

*The greater your desires, the dearer the price.*
*The more you hold on to, the more you'll lose.*

*Be content with what you have*
*and disgrace will not touch you.*
*Be satisfied with the way things are*
*and danger will be kept at bay.*
*Then your life will be everlasting.*
TAO TE CHING (#44)

# The We/They Syndrome

Charles has worked in the same business for thirty years and seems to get angrier and more closed down with every passing day. Charles makes lots of money—his reason for enduring the suffering. But even the money doesn't bring him much joy anymore. And the bitterness that pervades his work life spills over into the personal, so that even there his unhappiness is palpable. Charles's disdain (self-hatred disguised as justified anger) for his work is vociferously expressed, to anyone willing to listen, in antipathy and animosity toward his clients. It's him against them. He curses their incompetence and stupidity. Even the people on his side suffer his verbal abuse. He is the only one who does things right. If he could do it all himself, he'd have no problems. Other people are the reason he's so unhappy. No one that he comes in contact with in his work environment is spared his vitriol.

Most of us at one time or another have invoked the infamous *they*. We blame them for whatever discomfort we're experiencing or for not getting what we want.

Sometimes they don't even have a name or face. All we know is that *they* are not *we* or, even more specifically, *I*. Most of us don't let this syndrome overwhelm us to such an extent that we refrain from taking any responsibility at all. But employing this tactic in any way takes us away from ourselves and from the moment.

In Charles's case (an extreme example of the damage that can be wreaked) not only does he inhabit the we/they syndrome every day, but the anger that is generated by it permeates his whole life. He hates his work and the city he lives in. He is deeply angry and afraid—everyone who doesn't agree with him is bad or wrong, given that Charles can only see things in black and white. He's afraid that if he entertains ideas opposed to those he holds so dearly, his whole world will come crumbling down; that if he lets go of his attachment to money, all of it will disappear and he will have nothing; that he will lose what he has and not get what he wants. This syndrome has penetrated so deeply—right down to his core—that he even views women as *they*. He has not remarried since his first marriage fell apart more than twenty years ago because he doesn't want someone in his life who might take everything he has worked so hard for. Sharing the gifts of his abundant life is unthinkable. Sharing himself has become impossible.

Susan, on the other hand—who is in a work situation that almost invites the use of the we/they defense—has adopted a different strategy for dealing with the uncertainties of employment. Susan works in a small branch office of a major insurance company. The original company that hired her was sold to another some years ago, and rumors of being sold yet again run rampant. Other branch offices have folded, many people have moved on to other companies, and Susan and her one coworker are constantly under the threat of losing their jobs. It would be so easy here to point the finger in fear and say, "They are ruining my life. I wish they would just make a decision, or at least just let us know what's going on." Instead Susan has chosen to treat her work each day as if she were the boss, as if she owned the company and everything she produces matters. She doesn't focus on "what if they" or "can't they just"; she focuses on each day's work, its quality and her role in getting things done. As a result, she is content most days. She has accepted the idea that her job, as it is today, might not last forever, but she is proud of her work and feels good about her contribution. She couldn't work any differently even if she did own the company. And it is no coincidence that her office has been relatively untouched by all the main office's turmoil and shake-ups. Her supervisors notice her attitude and, more important to a bottom-line-driven company, her output. They have no reason to mess with a good thing.

Anytime we slip into the we/they vernacular our work suffers, and so do we, though our personal suffering is perhaps more subtle. It takes us away from the moment. Our attention to our work falters. The distraction allows our ego to slip in and question our circumstances. It is important to take notice when this happens and redirect our energy back to our work, away from the harmful influence of our ego-mind chatter. Absorbing ourselves in our work helps to quiet our mind and focus it on the task in front of us, which in turn creates an environment, internally and externally, in which we are most productive. This then makes us feel good about ourselves. And our efforts usually don't go unnoticed by others. When we pay attention to our own business, they will pay attention to theirs. The rest will happen as it happens.

---

1. How much of your energy, how much time in your day, is consumed by thoughts, fears and anxieties generated by the we/they syndrome? Reflect on this and make an attempt to write about it even if at first it doesn't seem to apply to you. Once you start writing you might be surprised at what comes up.

2. As you begin to become aware of when and why you do the we/they dance, try, each time you notice you're doing it, to bring your attention back around to you and what you're doing or not doing. Tell yourself that it's none of your business what they are or aren't doing.

3. If you don't already have a practice of meditation in your life, begin to set aside some time each day to sit quietly alone and concentrate on your breath. Even as little as ten minutes is enough to start, and everyone can find ten minutes in their day for themselves—even if it's behind a closed office door

during lunch. This is a perfect exercise to create balance in your day and help turn your focus away from them and toward you.

---

## Fear of Losing, Fear of Not Having

Sometimes we spend (or waste) so much time and energy worrying about losing something—our job, or the money we earn—that we might just as well not have it at all. Our fear makes it difficult to see what is real and what we truly want. It guides us into making decisions and doing things that we otherwise would not. We may never lose the fear completely, but if we allow it to determine our choices, it will become our constant companion. Nona's life exemplifies how fear can influence us, and then how we can overcome it.

Nona spent her twenties in a career that she fell into after college, one that she quickly realized did not suit her. Though she was successful in it, making good money with the promise of more, she decided to take a risk, leave her job, and return to school. She was young enough and responsible only for herself, so her fear was minimal. The future held many possibilities, even one of returning to her old career. She wasn't sure what she wanted to do with her life (fear kept her from acknowledging the one thing she knew she loved because it didn't seem to fit her definition of success), but she knew it wasn't what she was doing. She wanted to use her brain more and to do something creative.

Upon graduating, Nona still had no clear picture of the perfect career, but she entered a field that she grew to love. So her thirties were spent happily, in jobs that she liked. But always there was an underlying itch that something wasn't quite right, that it wasn't her true calling and didn't maximize her potential. Over the years Nona quietly explored her passion for photography. Relegating it to a hobby, she knew that it gave her life balance and meaning. Eventually her job, though she liked it well enough, simply became a means to support her art. Photography began to take up more and more of her time (she was even beginning to make a little money on small assignments for a few local newspapers), and her job became more of a hindrance than an aid. Each time she dreamt of leaving and making a living with photography, fear stopped her. Now in her forties, she realized her sense of time had changed and her financial responsibilities had grown. "I'm too old to start over. I have too many bills to pay. The field is crowded already, and I'm just an amateur; who would hire me?" No longer happy with her job, she became moody and depressed. Her work suffered. And the enthusiasm for her camera work waned.

When her annual review at work was less than stellar, Nona knew it was time to take action. She mustered up her courage and quit her job so that she could focus completely on her photography and try to make a decent living. She had some savings to help with the transition, and three years later she is still working for herself. It has not been easy, and fear often sets in—a few times Nona actually interviewed for a "real" job because the strain of making it on her own had become too great—but most days Nona wouldn't trade her current life for the old one. She realizes that she may never make the kind of money she once did, but she also knows that she is even happier with less. As Nona works through some of her money issues, she is certain that one day she'll have more than she ever dreamt. When she looks straight at her life without fear, she sees that she has everything she needs and, more important, everything she wants.

The fear is not completely gone, but it no longer has power over her. Nona simply acknowledges the fear and moves on to the next thing. Challenged by her chosen circumstances, Nona no longer lives in the future and what might happen there. If her life is proof of anything, it is that by doing what she loves, things just keep getting better and better.

---

1. Is there something that you're passionate about doing, that you'd love to do full time if you could? Even if it's been a secret up till now, or you think it would be impossible to make a living doing it, write about it. Write about your feelings, how long you've harbored this desire, what a typical day might look like if you were doing this thing. Let

yourself dream, but be sure to write it all down. It is important to do this in writing. Do not skip this step. Otherwise this dream will remain in your mind and never become a reality. Writing it down doesn't guarantee actualization, but it will bring you closer to it.

2. How much of a role does fear play in your life vis-à-vis work? Is it fear of losing, fear of not having, or both? If you're not already working in the field of your dreams, what are the fears that stop you? If you are in your chosen field but still unhappy, what fears are blocking you? Write about your fears, whatever they are, even if, especially if, fear is in your way.

---

## We Cannot Think Our Way to Understanding

Ever notice how the smarter someone is (and this may pertain to you), the less likely he or she is to be content with life, not to mention his or her lack of serenity? Sounds crazy, but our minds can interfere with our progress toward a happy, contented work life.

We are all conditioned to believe that our brain-power will determine our success. And to some extent this is true. In order to be skilled and competent in our work, we must employ our brains. But what happens too often is that we become creatures who are led around by our cerebral cortex. Our mind directs us and the rest of our being obediently follows. What we need to learn is that our bodies have a lot to teach us, and that everything cannot be understood in the usual conceptual way. This approach takes a huge leap of faith, since it runs contrary to what we've been taught, what we believe and how we've always operated in the world. But consider this: if we could *think* our way to happiness, wouldn't we already be there? Wouldn't we all be doing what we love and loving what we do? Wouldn't we be joyous and free every day? Thinking, then, does not hold the solution.

If you are dissatisfied in your work, it is not because you're incompetent, unlucky, not smart enough or even too smart. It is not because you haven't yet thought of the right approach to end your dissatisfaction. You do not have a problem with your thinking that needs fixing. What you have is a spiritual problem. And your spiritual center—the place that holds the solution—is not in your brain. Far from it. It is in your belly, in your body. So what you need to do is shift your focus and learn how to listen to what the voice of your spirit tells you. You have to learn to listen with your body, your intuition, your true nature. So rather than engage your brain, you must engage your breath, which is the only tool you need to build a centered, contented and happy work life.

So although you may not be able to think your way to understanding, you can get there by taking actions of a specific kind—actions that are simple no matter where on the scale of dissatisfaction you are, actions that will bring you close to your own personal truth, which will free you from self-will.

So how do all these things—self-will, breathing, thinking, taking action—relate? Very simply. In order to slow down our thinking, which is responsible for our confusion and dissatisfaction, and learn how to listen to our spiritual intuition, we must willfully take action *each day* and spend some time concentrating on our breath. This is the most important single step you can take toward reaching fulfillment in your work life.

---

1. Schedule (otherwise the time will disappear) at least fifteen minutes a day for some nonthinking breathing practice. (Fifteen minutes is good to start with, but after a few weeks this should increase to at least thirty minutes all at once or fifteen minutes twice a day. Once you begin to experience the benefits you will want to increase the time spent here to an hour or more. And one of the benefits of doing this exercise is that you will find more time in your day.)

2. Choose a time and a place where you can be relatively free of outside distractions. Sit in a position that will allow you to breathe deeply and fully. No slumping. Straighten your spine, loosen your belt. Lean on nothing. If you choose to sit in a chair, make it a straight-backed chair and sit away from the back, with your feet flat on the floor, hands resting gently in your lap. If you choose to sit on the floor, sit on a cushion, cross your legs, and let your knees fall to the floor. Be sure there is no

pressure on your ankles. Relax your head and let it sit squarely on your shoulders.

3. Keep your eyes gently open. This is important! Otherwise you will daydream or fall asleep.

4. Now just breathe. Bring all of your attention, your full concentration onto your breath. For the full length of the first exhalation, say the number one to yourself. For the second exhalation, say two. For the third exhalation, say three. And then begin again. One, two, three. Simple. Easy. Ultimately profound. When you do it, you will know this.

---

## Change Is in the Air

It's not only possible to be free of our dissatisfaction with work, it's actually quite simple. It is our desire for happiness that creates our unhappiness. So simply letting go of the desire will bring happiness. Sounds like a catch-22, except that it isn't. (Think about this: do you suppose that Joseph Heller set out to add a new word to our language when he wrote his war novel?) It is imperative to change our usual way of looking at things, and rather than looking outward to see what we can change, to bring us closer to what we want, we must look into ourselves to see what needs changing.

The point is not only that we can change but that we must. And in order for change to happen, you first need to be willing to change:

How you see things
How you do things
What you say
What you think
How you feel
How you don't feel
What you don't like
What you like
How you interact with others
What you believe

Because our grasp on the truth is tentative at best, we need to let go of our usual way of operating in the world and be open to a new way. This will strip away all the false supports that have been impeding us and interfering with our ultimate happiness. And this will expose the truth, the way things are, without illusion.

Change is in the air. Can you sense it? Feel it, smell it, taste it, embrace it. It is the only way—the only way to the extinction of desire, which causes so much pain.

Now, since you are willing to change, here is a simple exercise.

---

Read the following sentence and notice your reaction: *My unhappiness is preceded by and caused by my desire to be happy.*

Write down your feelings and thoughts about this. Does this idea confuse, frustrate, anger you? Why?

Now read the sentence again and don't react. Just read it. Breathe it in. Change the way you see it.

Finally, write about something concerning your work life that you're unhappy about. Then take away the desire to be happy. What's left? Write about that.

---

We are all looking for certainty. That is what our desire for happiness is. So whenever something good happens, we hold on to it for dear life, hoping it won't change. But we end up sucking the life out of it, and it eventually, and inevitably, turns bad. Or we grasp an ideal that will make us happy, and as we hold on for dear life, we are thrown around, battered and bruised by the forces of change. The only thing we can ever be certain of is change itself. So rather than struggle, if you accept that change surrounds you, you'll be freer and happier. You'll have no need to anchor yourself to anything, and you'll feel safe in the knowledge that all things change, including you, and including change itself.

---

Here's something to ponder in your new way of looking at things.

Bring to your mind an image of yourself when you were a young child of seven or eight. Compare that to who you are today. The adult you are now is very different, changed, from the child you were then. And that change happened slowly over time, with no two moments the same. In each moment over time you changed from what you were the moment before, and you did not remain that way the moment after, until you became who you are in this moment. And yet you are the same person. The adult is and yet isn't the child.

*Nothing is as it seems, nor is it otherwise.*

Do not try to figure this out. Just sit with it. If you sit with it long enough, without any expectation, the truth of it will be revealed. Remember: perseverance, endurance and, especially, patience.

---

## Accepting What Is

Mark is a talented musician who makes his living doing what he loves, playing and teaching music. But as Mark's experience will illustrate, this alone is not enough to guarantee happiness and contentment with work.

Mark has always made his living playing music, but because of the nature of that business there was never any security or consistent, dependable income. When Mark's daughter was born, he decided it was time to get a steady job with health insurance and a guaranteed paycheck. Since he was certified to teach, he took a job teaching music in one of his city's high schools. He never felt he was selling out because he loved exposing others to the joys of music, he knew he was a good teacher and he continued playing music with his band whenever possible. As a part-time father, he was able to devote many of his weeknights and weekends to playing music, and he was in much demand around town.

But the stress of having two careers, not to mention nurturing a relationship with a daughter who didn't live with him, began to take its toll on Mark's normally steady and upbeat nature. The abysmal conditions in his classroom only aggravated his state of mind. The high school he teaches in is fraught with troubles facing many city schools: lack of adequate funds, overcrowding and inattentive, uninterested students. Mark's classes are as large as fifty students, but attendance on any given day can be as low as 60 percent. This reduces the size of the class to thirty or forty students, which wouldn't be too bad, except for the lack of continuity. Whatever Mark covers on one day has to be repeated the next for those who were absent the day before. He was virtually unable to keep track of who knew what. The interested students became bored, the disinterested students generally remained that way, and Mark's level of frustration at being an ineffective teacher tormented him and affected more than his performance in the classroom. It began to seep into other parts of his life. He had trouble shaking off the mood that he felt his students and the educational system as a whole were responsible for.

But Mark knew he was in trouble and knew there must be a solution. He also knew the answer wasn't in trying to change the way his school operated and how his students learned. The solution to his frustration and disappointment lay within himself. So he took a risk and, fighting some major internal resistance, attended a weekend meditation retreat. He wanted answers to some questions that were plaguing him, most of which revolved around work, his effectiveness as a teacher, his future in music and his current frustration level. He wasn't sure he wanted to be responsible for the education of kids who not only didn't want to learn music but had behavioral and psychological problems that he was ill equipped to handle.

Mark's experience that weekend had a cathartic effect on his life. What he learned continues to resonate for him and inform his everyday life. At first Mark resisted the teachings offered that weekend (much like his own students), but he didn't walk away, and he finally opened to it. As soon as he did this and sat with the group in still silence his perspective and outlook began to shift. When Mark returned home he knew something was different, but he couldn't quite articulate it. He began to make some changes. The lessons of simplicity, patience and compassion that the quiet breathing and sitting-still exercises had taught him were immediately evident in some surprising ways. Mark began to simplify his physical space by clearing out and getting rid of stuff that cluttered his home. This external housecleaning is common after an initial exposure to a peaceful, serene environment, and it usually leads to housecleaning of a different sort—one that's internal and spiritual. When the space around and in us is cluttered, it is nearly impossible to hear and know our own truth. Intuitively, without being told, Mark knew this after his brief introduction to meditation. This began Mark's journey back to himself.

A year and a half later Mark is still teaching in the same school under the same conditions. But today he is no longer consumed with frustration and anger toward the system and his students. He continues to enjoy teaching and by his own admission is even better at it today. The biggest difference is that Mark no longer tries to change what he has no power to change. He doesn't give up on any student, and he lets them all know that he is there for each and every one of them. But he spends more time on those students who really want what he has to give and less time banging his drum, so to speak, in order to get the attention of the compulsively inattentive students. Mark accepts the way things are and has learned to work happily within this framework. He is a better teacher, his students gain more, and at the end of the day he is satisfied with his contribution.

When Mark was in the throes of his professional anguish, he searched for other teaching opportunities just to be out of the situation. Nothing happened. Now that he is more content (even though nothing changed on the outside) a recent opportunity for a more ideal teaching job was presented to him. Two years ago he would have jumped at the chance—for all the wrong reasons. Today he is more circumspect about it as he mindfully and judiciously reviews his career options. This offer has given him a chance to think about what he really and truly wants. And it may not involve teaching at all. But if he is offered this job and if he decides to take it, he will be there 100 percent, and for all the right reasons. He will not be running away from anything.

1. Are you in the business, profession or career of your choice but suffer frustrations and disappointment due to the environment, people or situation at work? Write about this. Be specific. (Even if you're not yet in your true calling, it is still important to do this exercise.)
2. Answer the following questions without thinking too much. Trust your first response.

   a. Are there things, situations and/or people at work that you would like to change?   YES   NO
   b. Write a list of the things you'd like to change and for each one respond to the following statement: *Realistically, I realize there is nothing I can do to change this.*

   *My List*

   _____   YES   NO
   _____   YES   NO
   _____   YES   NO
   _____   YES   NO
   _____   YES   NO
   _____   YES   NO
   _____   YES   NO
   _____   YES   NO
   _____   YES   NO
   _____   YES   NO
   _____   YES   NO
   _____   YES   NO

c. I would like to let go of the idea of changing these things and move on.    YES  NO

d. There is one thing, however, that I cannot let go of yet. It is _____.

e. I hope someday to be rid of this problem.    YES  NO

f. I can choose to let it go at any time.    YES  NO

3. Wherever you circled no, be aware that there is some resistance in you to seeing things as they are, to accepting what is, and that your frustration has little or nothing to do with outside circumstances. Once you realize this, you will be free and able to move on. So work on these areas. Think yes even if you don't yet mean it. Write yes. Don't allow the no to take charge.

---

# Quid Pro Quo

We all intuitively know what actions to take, what decisions to make, whom to trust, what to believe and so on. What is sometimes hard, though, is to be still and quiet long enough to hear this truth, to see the pearl amidst all the clutter that surrounds us, to sort through the confusion and reach a point of clarity. Carol's recent experience (and, in fact, her work history) will show us how everything is useful—even our so-called mistakes—and how all the clues for making hard decisions are clearly visible and audible if we follow our intuition.

Today Carol not only loves what she does, she loves having a job. She loves her boss and the people she works with, and she is well compensated. Not too long ago, however, she lost it all for a short time. Had it not been for some serious reflection, some knowledge of what her intuition actually is and a dose of fearlessness, she might have lost it forever.

Carol spent twelve years as a theatrical stagehand and loved her work. She left it only when it became clear that entry into the union that controls the industry was nearly impossible. And without a union job, she couldn't make a decent living wage. She sought out some professional help in redirecting her career and ended up going back to school to pursue a degree in imaging and photographic technology. Being in the right place (a technical college) at the right time (the years when the Internet first exploded) made Carol's future seem rosy. But it took her a year and a half to land a job after graduating, simply because she limited herself. She was trying to specialize in a very small field when all the signs around her were suggesting that she give up that idea. Finally, as soon as she decided that she could be a generalist, she got a job as an Internet project manager for a large media company. Not only were her newly acquired technical skills important for doing the job but the experience of staging large theatrical shows helped immensely. And she loved it! She found herself in a job that previously she could not have imagined for herself, especially when she had been so intent on specializing. This job suited her experience and personality to a T. Then the bottom fell out.

The company reorganized, her department disbanded, her boss resigned and three to five people were leaving every week. Carol felt as though she were on a sinking ship. She wanted to stay—the company wasn't asking her to leave, and she still liked it—but it was getting more difficult for her to do her job. Then fear set in. She started interviewing for other jobs. She decided that she wanted to be an Internet person in an Internet company. She received two job offers in the first week. She was lured by the promise of future money—stockoptions, frequent future raises and so on. Her company counteroffered with more money and a better job. However, in a meeting she got the sense that they weren't committed to the segment of the business that she was in. Fear intruded again.

Carol took one of the job offers. She knew immediately it was the wrong decision, but she gave notice anyway. She didn't want to leave. She liked the company, and even though they begged her to stay she declined. Something told her it was the responsible thing to do— she had accepted the new job offer and felt she had to follow through.

Throughout this whole process Carol was confused, and every conversation she had with friends and family revolved around this issue. She was faced with one of the biggest decisions of her life and didn't know how to make that decision. She talked to people about it and asked for help. But she knew that ultimately it was her own decision. So she meditated on it even when her mind refused to quiet down. She spent time alone listening for the answer. And she waited for the intuitive pull in her gut. Somehow her signals got crossed; she made her choice and didn't realize until later that experiencing so much pain after making a decision meant that something was wrong.

From the first moment of her first day in her new job, she was aware that she had made a mistake. As Carol tells it: "I felt like I was going against my grain every day. I felt I had to sell my soul, my life. People there were miserable and overworked. I kept saying to myself, 'This is not for me. This is not where I belong.'" Although she thought it, she was unable to say out loud, "I've changed my mind. I've made the biggest mistake of my life." But after the second miserable week she knew she couldn't stay. What was getting harder and harder to live with was the knowledge and understanding that she had gone against her gut instinct, her intuition, when she took the job. She hadn't honored the voice inside that said, "If you're this unhappy about a decision, it's wrong." Carol was extremely lucky when she called her former company at the end of two weeks and they invited her back. After three weeks she gave notice. At the end of five, she departed and returned to her old company. But in those five weeks and in the weeks leading up to this time, she learned some valuable lessons. And she even has a better job now than if she had stayed put.

Carol sees her decision to leave her company and take a new job as *wrong*. But was it really? We could turn it around and say that because of the way things turned out it was the *right* decision. After all, she not only has a better job and is making more money than if she had stayed, she also acquired a few new skills along the way. But rather than calling it right or wrong, let's just call it Carol's decision. It was the best she could do at the time, and there is no right or wrong about it—it just is what it is. Surely Carol will face many difficult decisions as her career progresses. The important thing for her to remember, and what we all can learn from her example, is that she knows the answer already; all she has to do is listen hard enough to uncover it and trust it when it rises to the surface.

## Freedom from Anxiety and Fear

Have you ever stopped to consider what it is that actually creates or causes anxiety? Once you admit fear, have you ever taken note of the source of that fear? Chances are the reasons, whatever they are, don't reside in the present moment. Chances are both the fear and the anxiety are connected to some past event that your mind can't let go of or some future event that you have no way of predicting. So the only solution, the only way to eradicate fear and anxiety, is to keep yourself in the present moment—away from both the past, which is over, and the future, which has not yet happened.

If you've come this far and if you've done the suggested exercises, the idea of living in the present moment will not seem revelatory. It will seem as natural as breathing. And in fact it is our breathing that will not only inform us how anxious or fearful we are but heal us, bring us back to ourselves and help us to once and for all be rid of our fears and anxieties.

Our emotional states are reflected in our breathing. Shallow breathing signals stress of some sort—anxiety, fear, anger—while deep, relaxed breathing signifies contentment and inner peace. Which comes first, the breathing or the feeling? Like the chicken-and-egg question, does it really matter? They are linked and cannot exist without each other. So then logically we can conclude that if one changes, so will the other. If we move from an excited, fearful state to a more relaxed one, our breathing will shift from shallow to deep. Wouldn't it then follow that if we change our breathing, we will change our mood? The answer is a resounding yes! But all you skeptics out there might need proof. And the proof is in the doing. So let's do it. Only when you experience the power you have in your breath will you be convinced that it's possible to gain freedom from the emotions, ideas and values that imprison you, strangle you and keep you in a dissatisfied state.

## BREATH EXERCISE #1:
## NOTICING YOUR BREATH

*Where in your chest does your breath reside? Sit up straight with your feet flat on the floor and close your eyes. Bring your full attention to your breath. Concentrate completely on one full breath. Notice your inhalation—feel the air enter through your nostrils. Follow your breath as it fills your lungs. Then follow your exhalation as your chest deflates. Notice how deep your breath goes. Now, without changing the way you breathe, spend a few more moments with your eyes closed, noticing each inhalation and each exhalation. Do nothing else. Just breathe and pay attention to it.*

## BREATH EXERCISE #2:
## BALLOON BREATHING

*Sitting up straight, with your feet flat on the floor, close your eyes and bring your full attention to your breath. Imagine that inside your chest cavity is a large, deep cup. As your breath enters your body, imagine this cup filling up with air, from the bottom to the top. As you exhale, picture the air flowing out of this cup from the top down. Exaggerate your in-breath and your out-breath so that you slowly and deliberately fill up and then empty this cup. Do this eight or ten times. Then replace the cup with an upside-down balloon and repeat the exercise. Inflate and then deflate this balloon inside your chest. Do this eight or ten times slowly, with your eyes closed and all of your attention and complete concentration on this exercise.*

*Then open your eyes and continue this slow, rhythmic filling of the balloon. Look down at your torso as you do it. Watch your chest expand and contract as you breathe this way. Feel where in your chest cavity the bottom of the cup or balloon sits. How deep is it? Put your palm on that exact spot and continue breathing this way for a few more moments. Then slowly return to normal breathing and notice what, if anything, has changed.*

---

Write about this breath experience. Take note of your state of mind. What was it before and then after this exercise? Any difference? How about the state of your body? Is there more or less tension? In writing about all of this you will observe your mind. Rather than having your mind control you, just observe it. Be your own silent witness to the workings of your mind. Observe your breath to observe your mind, and your truth will reveal itself. And there will be no fear.

---

BREATH EXERCISE #3:
EXTENDED BALLOON BREATHING

*Sit up straight with your feet flat on the floor and bring your attention to your breath. Close your eyes for a few moments and slowly inflate and deflate the imaginary balloon in your chest. Notice how just a few moments of this deep breathing calms and centers your body and mind.* (You can do this centering breath exercise anywhere, anytime, especially when you're feeling anxious, impatient, worried or frightened.

Try it the next time you are about to face something or someone that creates such feelings—the next time your boss calls you into his or her office, for instance—and you'll be surprised how much calmer you'll be.)

*Place your open palm at the bottom of the balloon and then move your palm down a few inches, just below the base of your breath. Then, on the next exhalation, extend your out-breath, and with that exhalation elongate the balloon so that it reaches the center of your palm. Then continue inhaling and exhaling, inflating and deflating, with the balloon, with your breath, now deeper into your body. Breathe this way for a few moments, eight or ten breaths, with your eyes closed and then for eight or ten breaths with your eyes open.*

---

You can do this exercise throughout the day, anytime you have a free moment, anytime you feel stressed or anxious. The purpose of it is to loosen your diaphragm and deepen your breath so that you naturally breathe from a place other than your throat or upper chest. Anytime you notice that your breath is in your throat or you are having trouble catching your breath or you are holding your breath, you can be sure that something is going on. But there is an immediate and, if you practice it often, long-term cure. Concentrated balloon breathing—it's a miracle that we can all perform at will.

All of these breathing exercises are ones that you will come back to again and again. Keep practicing them. Practice one or all of them at least once a day. These last two are the hardest of all, but your practice will prepare you for them. If you're a goal-oriented person (and who of us isn't to some extent?), consider these your goal. And you may not even want to try them until you master the other ones—until your whole diaphragm is relaxed and flexible.

---

BREATH EXERCISE #4:
BELLY BREATHING, PART I
*Part I is rather easy and can be done at any time. It is yet more practice for the more difficult Part II.*

*Lie on your back on the floor. A carpet, mat or flat blanket under your whole body is a good idea. You can also use your bed or sofa, but the floor is ideal. For a few moments close your eyes and scan your body, relaxing it as you move your attention from your toes to the top of your head. Take your time with this. Have your legs out straight on the floor. If there's too much strain on your lower back, place a pillow under your knees or bend your knees and place your feet flat on the floor. Wear loose clothing and no shoes to do this exercise. Have your arms down by your sides, palms up. Just breathe and relax your body. Notice where there is stress and breathe into each of those places. Notice your breath. Bring your attention to your breath and notice the difference in your body as you inhale and then as you exhale. Feel the weight of your body on the floor, the pull of gravity.*

*Now place the palms of your hands on your belly—the soft area just below your navel. Imagine a balloon in this area that inflates as you inhale and deflates as you exhale. Breathe into this balloon, expanding and contracting your belly as you breathe. Do this eight or ten times and then relax your breath*

*and breathe normally, keeping your hands in place on your belly.
As you breathe normally, feel the movement of your belly. You
should feel at least a slight rising and falling of your belly
even without forcing it. Just relax and enjoy that feeling for a
few moments, the natural rhythm of your body as you breathe.*

*As an experiment, after you feel somewhat or, better yet,
completely relaxed think of something that troubles you and then
notice how this thought affects your breath, your body, your
relaxed state. Do you feel your belly tighten, your breath move
higher into your body? Did you momentarily hold your breath?
Did you experience shortness of breath? Simply take note of how
even the smallest thought or slightest feeling changes the depth
and rhythm of your breathing.*

---

As children, we all breathe naturally from our bellies.
If you can, watch a small child breathe while at rest.
Most likely you will notice what you just felt in your
own body: the gentle rising and falling of the belly, naturally and spontaneously. But what happens to us over
the years is that we fill up this space with grief, anger,
fear and sorrow, and it disallows this natural breathing
rhythm. Our breath moves up our body, and the more
we store the higher it goes. Our diaphragm tightens,
and we breathe from our upper chest and throat. So your
job here is to move your breath down deeper into your
body so that you can release the fears and anxieties
trapped there. It takes time and it takes practice, but it's
possible. And not only will you get rid of all the junk
that you've accumulated, but your health will improve

and your mind will clear up. What you are left with is your truth. And with that, anything is possible.

---

BREATH EXERCISE #5:
BELLY BREATHING, PART II

*Sit up straight, feet flat on the floor. Maintain the natural curve to your spine, and let it, rather than a wall or the back of a chair, hold you erect. Close your eyes and spend a few minutes on the balloon breathing, drawing your breath down deep and relaxing your diaphragm. Now, place your open palms on your belly as you did in Part I, and feel how relaxed or tight your belly is. Then exaggerate your breath and fill up the imaginary balloon that's in your belly as you inhale, deflating it as you exhale. Do this eight or ten times. You'll probably notice that it's not quite so easy to do when sitting up.*

*Then relax your breath and breathe normally, but keep your attention in your belly as you concentrate on your breath. Breathe from your belly.*

---

Because of the accumulated stuff that resides in our belly, the longer we sit, the more this stuff will reassert itself and send our breath upward. But, paradoxically, the longer we sit, the more chance we have of always breathing from our bellies and ridding ourselves of this stuff forever. So practice breathing, practice sitting, practice concentrating. And then freedom, freedom and more freedom will be the happy result.

# This Is It!

Let's review what you've rediscovered in this third step of realization.

1. You saw how much of your energy is directed outward toward others and how much of a role fear plays in your everyday work life. With this, you've begun to realize that the only solution to any dilemma you face is to look toward yourself.

2. You realized that establishing a daily ritual of quiet reflection and meditation is necessary for a balanced and harmonious existence.

3. You recognized that change is inevitable, that all things change, and so must you. If you are resistant and stuck, you must look within to get unstuck.

4. You acknowledged that living in the present, rather than the past or the future, and accepting what is, is your only chance for serenity.

5. Your intuition holds your truth. You saw how it is only fear and your inability to listen well that keep you from it.

6. You experienced how your breath can be your guide and lead you into a healthy and balanced life, in and out of work.

The realization that this is it, that the present moment is all there is and that it holds our truth and all the answers, may not yet have hit you. Sometimes this realization takes time to seep in. It's not so easy to realize that right now, at this moment, we have all we need and that everything is as it should be, especially when we're experiencing any sort of discomfort or difficulty. It's much easier for us to think, "It's possible, but it's just not here yet." The truth, though, is that it's here now, right in front of us, and has been all along. Sometimes it hits us like a ton of bricks and we experience that *aha!* moment when all the pieces click into place. Other times it's a gradual awakening, and little by little the truth dawns on us, until one morning we are so steeped in it we can't even recall the moment of transition.

Consider that this truth, this perfect existence, is a mountain, and we are on a path toward this mountain. There is a path; there is a mountain. The path leads us to the mountain, but the mountain is not the result of the path. The mountain is there and always has been. The path simply brings us to it. And it is in the next part of the book, in steps four to seven, that this path will be elucidated. This path that will lead you to your truth, the truth that is already there.

> *My words are easy to understand*
> *and easy to put into practice.*
> *But if you try to understand their meaning*
> *and try to practice them,*
> *you will fail.*
>
> *So put your intellect aside*
> *and look inside your heart.*
> *Only then will you know.*
>                TAO TE CHING (#70)

# THE PATH

Once we come to understand and accept the truth of our discontent (step one) and then look closer at the causes (step two), we can more easily grasp the notion that not only can there be an end to it but the end is possible right here, right now (step three). If you've done the work of these steps, this would be a good time to go back to the two questions posed at the very beginning of this process, to take note of how your responses have changed so far: *Is your work nature different and separate from your nature outside work? Is your job, your work, the cause of your dissatisfaction, or does the source lie elsewhere?*

Spend at least ten minutes on each of these questions, writing about your current reaction to them. Take that time right now or it will disappear. These are important funnels into self-discovery, so it will benefit you to make the effort.

One thing you may have noticed so far is how interrelated everything is. There doesn't seem to be a really clear separation and distinction between the first three steps in this process, for instance. One flows into the next and back again, as the lines between them blur. If you're like most people, you probably would prefer a clear beginning, middle and end, a logical step-by-step process that moves you along toward the prize, the reward, the result of your efforts. This seven-step process is not so linear. But the rewards are plentiful. If you honestly and diligently take the suggestions outlined here, you will be happier at work, you will love what you do and do what you love, you will enjoy daily contentment and peace and you will put the past behind you and not worry about the future. You will be free from fear and anxiety, from selfish desire and pride, and be filled with tolerance, love and understanding. And you don't have to wait until the end to begin enjoying these fruits. They are yours even now. Don't worry if you feel as though you don't yet have a firm grasp on steps one, two and three. The next four steps will help you gain a fuller understanding. And if you adopt steps four to seven as a way of life, then steps one to three will become clearer. There is fluidity to this process, just as there is to life. It is unpredictable, ungraspable and impermanent. If you expect otherwise, you will be disappointed. If you remain rigid, you will be torn apart.

Together let's explore the subject of our nature in and out of work. We may have to don a particular suit of clothes, a prescribed set of behaviors and a certain attitude when we present ourselves at work. And we may think that this makes us a different person from the one we are at home and with friends. But just as we can't change the basic color of our eyes, we are at our core the same person at work as at home. And even if we attempt to draw firm boundaries between them, since we, the common denominator, are moving back and forth across this line, we can't help but carry parts of our lives back and forth. There is an interrelationship here that can't be avoided.

Thinking that there is a specific set of rules determining our behavior at work and that these rules differ from those we abide by at home is a delusionary notion, one that merely helps us to justify and rationalize bad behavior. So while the steps here address your work life, they also pertain to your whole life. If you behave well at work, if you're happy there, then the same will be true outside of work and vice versa. A friend of mine claims that he can tell what sort of a businessperson someone is by playing a round of golf with him. Along with his business manner, he reveals what sort of parent, spouse and friend he is as well. As much as we think we can compartmentalize the various parts of our lives, in the end it is impossible; there is always seepage.

Steps four to seven offer you a way of life, a path that will lead you toward freedom and happiness. They are specifically targeted to work but can and should be adopted for your whole life. Remember that all of this is a process that invites practice. Some of the suggested actions here are tall orders. Some of them will be difficult to adhere to 100 percent of the time, especially as you come up against ingrained and habitual patterns. And some of them will seem rather prosaic and predictable. But if you approach them all wholeheartedly, and if you exercise thoroughness and diligence, you will reap the promised rewards even before you finish. For, in fact, you are never truly finished—and if you're honest with yourself, wouldn't that seem pretty dull anyway? Enjoy the adventure here. Live with your heart open to the world around you and take in all that is offered, for none of it will ever be the same again.

## The Fourth Step
# BALANCE

■

The manner in which we conduct ourselves determines not only the impression we make but also what we ultimately think and feel about ourselves. Our behavior speaks volumes. When it comes to work we often believe that we can survive and succeed with our intellect and/or talent alone. This erroneous notion causes a serious imbalance that leads many of us down a one-way dead-end road. We cannot be whole and happy if we operate with only half of our faculties engaged. So it is imperative that we develop both our intellect and our heart in equal measure, or risk a life half lived.

Most especially at work, where intellectual development is rather easy, we need to nurture our compassionate heart side. At home it might be just the reverse. We can fool ourselves into thinking that engaging our intellect at work and our heart at home creates balance. But if we listen for just a moment to what our intuition might say about that, or even what our experience tells us, we know at once that this idea is not only false but foolish. Switching parts of ourselves on and off, depending on the circumstances, is difficult at best. It makes much more sense and delivers much more contentment to merge the two and have no need to be a different person at work than we are at home. Certainly the demands are different and tap into different aspects of our personalities and skills, but when our core self is stable and true we never have to wonder what the appropriate behavior might be. When we develop an ethical mode of behavior there is no question of what to do next or how to handle a baffling situation. Our moral spine will move us forward with strength, stability and balance. The ethics and morals that we live by are not those imposed by anything or anyone outside of us. They are and should be determined by us and our own sense of truth. And that, as you know by now, can be heard in the quiet of the breath.

If at this point in your search for enjoyment and contentment with work you've come to the realization that the answer is not simply in what you do for a living—though that is important, as we shall see—but in how you do it, congratulations. And if you've also accepted the idea that it is your spiritual development that you must work on to achieve a gratifying work life, then more kudos to you. If you're still grappling with these concepts, do not despair. Keep going. A gradual awakening to these principles often results in a deeper embodiment of them. And once you see that your happiness is contingent upon your spiritual development you soon come to know that this must have a moral foundation. In other words, when you are spiritually grounded you know to do the right thing in matters big and small. And doing the right thing—ethical conduct—encompasses what you actually do for a living, how you behave each day and what you say. There is no one judging you or rating your performance here. There are no shoulds or oughts. But there are suggestions of what constitutes moral and ethical behavior. We'll explore how your behavior impacts on the quality of your life and your day-to-day satisfaction. Like everything else here, you make the decision about what works for you and what doesn't. By now you've begun to trust yourself more. At the end of the day only you know if you did the right thing. You have to live with the consequences of your behavior.

*Understanding others is knowledge,*
*understanding yourself is wisdom.*
*Conquering others takes force,*
*conquering yourself takes strength.*

*To know contentment is to be rich.*
*To move forward with purpose is to have ambition.*
*To be sure of one's place is to endure.*
*To embrace death is to live a long life.*

TAO TE CHING (#33)

# Doing the Right Thing

If you're unhappy with your chosen profession, it's necessary to step outside of it for a while in order to make an impartial assessment. (This needs to be done even before you investigate whether or not you've actually made the choice to be where you are. That we'll look at later.) So first things first. Take a look at your industry. Pretend that you are an outsider. This will afford you a clear picture of what it is that you do and what effect your work has on the world around you. There may be factors at play affecting your work satisfaction that prior to such an investigation were not clear to you but had their effect nonetheless.

It may be obvious, but when we work for a company that pollutes the environment, for instance, not only are we, as individuals in the company, responsible, but the cumulative effect that this behavior has on our psyche, our spiritual development and our ultimate happiness is quite potent. When we pollute the rivers, streams and wildlife around us, we end up polluting ourselves and our loved ones as well. Most of us would probably agree that polluting the environment for profit is at the least unethical.

Let's start, then, with the most important question regarding the ethical nature of our work.

1. *Does my company/industry/profession cause harm to others?* Write about this and be honest with yourself. Remember that here in this exercise you are an impartial observer.

WORK FROM THE INSIDE OUT

Don't let worry interfere with your judgment. You might ask what exactly "cause harm to others" means? Here are some suggestions. A company causes harm if it trades or manufactures lethal weapons, produces or sells harmful intoxicants and/or poisons, engages in the practice of killing living creatures, or cheats, lies and deceives people.

Most of us are not employed in such commerce. But there are many other subtler ways in which companies can harm their customers and employees. If your company engages in questionable practices generally, the best move would be to seek employment in a more honorable company or profession. If you walk away, your bravery will inspire others to do the same. And if we all conduct our individual lives in an ethical and moral manner, then our behavior will ripple through society and effectively drown out the dishonorable professions. Sometimes, though, corruption and negligent practices are systemic and simply "the way things are," seemingly beyond saving or changing. Drastic measures may then be called for, because, as we've learned, anything can change, and it is our responsibility to effect change if it is at all in our power.

The tobacco industry is a perfect example of how harmful practices can become commonplace and accepted, how such practices can corrupt many intelligent people and then how one person's courage can explode the deception and denial. Not many of us are in a position to be a whistle-blower, nor would we want to be. But even when such extreme measures are called for, even when such actions may temporarily rip our life apart, in the end we are always better off.

2. *What good does my company do? Am I proud to be a part of it?* If you are unhappy at work and can't yet muster up some pride, be the impartial observer again and consider your company's profile. See it as one small part of the larger whole. And even if it seems that your company is only interested in making money (so many companies, even nonprofit ones, are fixated on the bottom line these days), there is nothing inherently wrong with that unless it brings harm to others. If your company's product or service is money, there is value in that. If it is some other product or service and you believe that quality has been compromised in order to make money, ask yourself what harm it's causing and then feel the effect.

Do you even know your company's purpose or main goal? Does it have a mission statement? If you don't know, find out. Get to know your company better. Learn its philosophy of doing business. Do your research. Write about the product or service that your company offers. How do you feel about it? Can you see where it helps people rather than harms them? Write a list of the good things your company does and then look at each one. Discover the pleasure in being involved with these. Keep the big picture in sight as you observe your contribution to the whole.

3. *How do I feel about the industry in general that I work in?* Again, put on your hat of impartiality and look objectively at your industry. If you've been so miserable in it, this will certainly be challenging, but every honor-

able industry contributes something. It is your job here to identify and describe what that is. To paint a balanced picture you may also include its deficiencies. Be honest and fair. Try not to stretch the truth either way. And remember, nothing is perfect.

Engaging in right livelihood is crucial to our spiritual well-being and our sense of balance in the world. What is right for one person may not be ultimately right for another. But any profession that does not harm others is right livelihood. If your path is to leave the industry you're in and immerse yourself in another that feels more right for you, before you go or make any changes embrace whatever it is that you do today and let yourself be proud of doing it. Then, if you must, you can walk away with a clear conscience. This is your life. You are where you are for a reason. Respect that. Honor that. And then, wherever you are, you will be proud and happy.

---

1. Once you've identified the good that your company does, the contribution it makes to society, let your own contribution to that effort be your motivation and source of pride. For one week, each day before setting off to work, establish your intention for that day. Let your reason for showing up be what you are doing for others. Do not—for this week—concern yourself with what you are getting back. Simply be content for this short time to go to work thinking of and helping others. Each

time anger or resentment crops up and you begin to focus on what you are or aren't getting, take your attention away from yourself and direct it toward others. Consider this week to be your service commitment to society.

2. At the end of the week (and even daily if you have the time) write about this experience. Were you happy and satisfied with work most of the week, or were you sitting in misery? What was different? How did this approach to work change your outlook toward your industry, your company, or the work that you do?

3. If after evaluating your industry and your company, defining its role in society and its contribution to the good you are still dissatisfied because its goals do not match closely enough with your own, then it may be time to move on. But before you do, be sure to do your homework and don't get caught grabbing at some opportunity merely for the superficial perks. Decide first which industry and which company is most compatible with your personal moral outlook. Start with that, because if you do, all the other factors will fall into place—the salary, the benefits, the job itself. If you don't feel good about what you're about to do each day when you head off to work, then no amount of money or other compensation will make up for this lack.

4. If with these exercises you've come to appreciate and respect the industry and company you're in

but are still unhappy with the job you have, then there's more work to be done. Appraise your job objectively. Take yourself out of the picture and with clear vision look at the job itself. Write about it. How does it contribute to the company's goals? Is it a necessary and valuable position in the big picture? Or is the job superfluous, redundant and unnecessary? If this is the case, do not take it personally. This is not about you yet. This is about the job. Here are three possible scenarios:

a. By divorcing yourself emotionally from the job you can see its value. You see how your contribution benefits the whole. A sense of pride is born. You return to your job with renewed energy and commitment, leaving aside the petty and selfish demands that previously bogged you down. You look forward once again (or for the first time) to going to work.

b. You learn to see the value in the job but realize that it is not one that you are best suited for. You begin to see that your negativity has resulted in missed opportunities. You vow to change your attitude, express pride in your work and work toward the job you really want, without denigrating the job you already have. With your new on-the-job conduct you will send the message in a clear, strong voice that you are a valuable worker. You will feel good about yourself and your output. And your company will end up doing the right thing as well. You begin to see that this is a serious relationship that goes both ways.

c. In your job analysis your worst fear is realized. It becomes apparent that your position in the company is superfluous. The job that you do—or at least 80 to 90 percent of it—is redundant or unnecessary. You see how this has eaten away at your self-pride, as you've pretended along with others that what you do is important. Before resorting to worry and fear, first realize that this is not your fault and trust that this is good news. Then decide that taking some action to rectify the situation will give you back some self-esteem. Write a report to your superiors outlining your findings. You will be rewarded—perhaps not in the way you expect, but rewarded nonetheless. And you will be happier. So trust that if you do the right thing here, the right thing will happen for you. Be open-minded and honest and you won't be disappointed.

---

When we are engaged in honorable work, in right livelihood, then one piece to the big puzzle of job satisfaction and loving what we do falls into place. This alone does not guarantee happiness, but it is a necessary ingredient. If we can't hold our head up at the end of the day and be proud of the work we do, then that happy-with-work feeling will elude us.

Sometimes you may not readily be able to put your finger on what is wrong. That's why a thorough investigation of all the factors that could account for your dissatisfaction is important. So until you take an objective look at the industry, company and job that you're in (one factor), you will never be sure of the cause. And whenever there is confusion, frustration and disaffection are not far behind. So it is important to understand and accept that if your company participates in questionable practices, you in turn are affected, even if you don't engage in the dishonorable conduct yourself. Ignoring the reality won't make it go away or change its effect. Once you know, then you can move on. Educating yourself in every way about every aspect of your vocation will help to strengthen the foundation of balance that is so crucial to a fulfilling work life.

## Ethical and Moral Actions

Once we assess the big picture—the ethics of our industry and company—then we must turn the mirror around and observe our own day-to-day behavior at work. As we learned earlier, everything that we do has an effect, and the fullest effect falls on us. Here we will notice the powerful impact our behavior has on our state of mind, and we will learn that through taking action of a different sort we can effect change and get closer to enjoying each and every day that we show up for work.

Do you think the set of rules prescribing your behavior at work and that prescribing it outside of work are the same or different?

Write about this for a few minutes and describe the similarities and the differences. Be specific.

At this moment you may want to skip the above exercise and just keep reading, with the good intention of returning to it, but I urge you to do it now. Even if you have the answer in your mind clearly and distinctly, or if you think the answer doesn't mean all that much and you're reading this to learn new things, consider this: it is imperative that you write down your own response to this question, and all the others presented to you in this book. In the end neither I nor anyone else can teach you anything when it comes to spiritual matters (and work is a spiritual matter). We can only guide you toward your own truth. Writing things down brings clarity of mind and thought. It removes the clutter from our brains and leads us to a more serene place. (Serenity is a condition of mind and body together that allows us to be fully present, aware and awake in each moment, ready for whatever comes our way and not distracted by any internal or external factors. This is a much-needed quality in the work environment, conducive to deep concentration and high productivity.) Writing also offers us a few surprises and a deeper insight into ourselves. When we write things down, see it in black and white and then reread what we've written, we usually gain a keener understanding of what we actually think and how we feel, and the confusion about what to do next subsides. The page in front of us is a blank slate, a broad canvas on which to deposit everything, and so the smaller, softer, quieter thoughts and feelings in our mind that have been hiding behind or dominated by our loud and perhaps obsessive thoughts will finally have their voice heard. So write for yourself, to express those gentle (and sometimes not-so-gentle) thoughts. Now, with all of that said, if you decide to skip over this writing exercise and continue on, that's okay too.

Before you go on to the next few questions, take a few moments to do the following exercise. Sit up straight and take a few deep breaths, concentrating only on your breath. Refer to the breathing exercises on pages 132–137 if you need a refresher. With your eyes closed, bring your attention to your internal judge/critic. Try to visualize what this looks like and where in your body it sits. Maybe it resides on your shoulder or deep in your gut. Wherever it is (and if you don't have one, consider yourself lucky), imagine removing it for the time being and placing it outside your front door. (You will be able to pick it back up the next time you go out.) Now do the same thing with your internal saint and any other voice that you know was imported and is not generated from within you. This can be tricky because we often live with something so long we cannot be sure if it's our own voice or not. For this exercise remove the ones that are obviously not yours, along with the judge and saint even if you think they are you.

This exercise may arouse certain emotions and stimulate thought. Please take the time now to write about the effect of this exercise before moving on. Take advantage of every opportunity to learn more about yourself and how you operate in the world. Pay attention to both the input and your output.

---

Have you ever stolen something from a store, friend or family member? Have you ever wanted to?

Do you use company supplies (pens, paper, copiers, faxes, phones, computers, etc.) for your personal use?

Do you cheat on your expense account?

Do you misrepresent your income and expenses to the IRS?

If you do any of these things do you justify your actions with "They can afford it," "I deserve it," "They expect it," "It's our unspoken agreement, a little bonus," "Everyone does it"?

Do you watch others do these things and sit in judgment of them?

---

If these questions make you uneasy (even with your judge and saint removed), I can assure you that you're not alone. Chances are that most of us have stolen, cheated, lied or judged at some point in our lives, and most likely the forum was the workplace. (Although if we do it there, we're more likely to do it elsewhere as well.) Why do you suppose we, who wouldn't dream of stealing outside of work, think nothing of taking from our employer? How is it that we rarely call this stealing or even petty theft, and only when it reaches huge proportions, such as embezzlement, do we pay attention? Ask yourself why this is and how you feel about it. Is it right or wrong to steal from our employer, to cheat on our expense account? Is it right or wrong to embezzle money or steal a car? Putting the legal differences aside, let's just pay attention to the ethical and moral implications. And then let's take a moment to ask a few other questions: *Why is it that when the discussion turns to ethics and morality we tend to groan and want to walk away? And why does being good have such a bad rap today?*

Every human being has the capacity to be both good and bad. So if we agree that this is true, and if we agree that stealing a pen is not exactly good (and therefore must be bad) and embezzling the company's money is bad (and has no good in it), then the difference is only a matter of degree. And while you might argue that stealing a pen hurts no one, I would argue that it does indeed hurt someone: you. Though you may be able to live with this and may never escalate your tendency to steal a pen into committing a felony, it is important for you to admit that given the right circumstances, the right pressures and the right opportunity you are at least capable of such behavior.

There are a few reasons why it is important to recognize this. First, it helps you to look honestly at your behavior and to establish your parameters of ethical conduct. It forces you to discontinue your rationalizations for minor transgressions and to see the truth of things. It also teaches you how powerfully destructive, insidious and subtle denial can be. And perhaps most important, when you admit that anything is possible and that you can choose what to do and what not to do, you develop compassion toward yourself and others. And the reason why it is so important to be compassionate is because this quality, side by side with wisdom, creates a harmonious balance in our lives. And remember, your judge and saint are not on the scene, are not witnessing this, so no matter what you reveal here, what behavior you admit to, you will not be judged or punished. All of this is an exercise that will bring you closer to your truth, nurture your compassion and give you a platform from which you can operate with a clear conscience, a moral spine and an ethical code of conduct. These are important if you want to experience contentment and satisfaction in your work each and every day.

Deciding to behave in an ethical way at work and to refrain from "borrowing" stuff from our employer and judging others is not such a difficult task. We can immediately put this pledge into action and reap the rewards. Our conscience will be clear and we will like ourselves more. This in turn will allow us to confront whatever anger toward our employer or ourselves motivated us to steal in the first place. And rather than sublimate our true feelings, everything will be aboveboard and we will face every challenge as it arises. But sometimes we are confronted with situations where either the right action is not so obvious or we think it will compromise our job security or reputation. What then?

Once we begin to disengage from our bad behavior (and starting with the small things makes it easier) our sense of propriety sharpens. And along with being able to detect improprieties, we also become quite adept at knowing how to handle them. If it is a thorny issue, make no rash decisions. Sit with it for a while, ask for help from those you trust. Pray about it and sit some more. The answer will be revealed to you. You will know what to do. Sometimes the right thing is not the easy thing. Sometimes your ego will throw a little tantrum when it realizes the right action that must be taken. But you will know what to do. Trust yourself. And the more right actions you take, the more confident you will become. You may find yourself going against the grain. When you do, be sure not to judge those going in the other direction. Have compassion for them. Be an example for them to follow without becoming self-righteous, and some of them will follow. Just keep doing the right thing, and the repercussions of your behavior will be felt far and wide.

While we're on the topic of right action in the workplace, we must not overlook a sensitive issue that often makes headlines: sexual relations in the workplace. We are all human. And just as we cannot completely separate our work persona from our persona outside of work, we cannot expect to become asexual beings during work hours. We do not have an on/off switch for our hormones. When we work eight or more hours a day with the same people, we are bound to develop intimate bonds, and from this may arise sexual attraction. However, while it is only human to feel this way—a condition we should not judge or punish ourselves for—we do have a choice of what to do with such feelings. The right action is no action. Sex does not belong at work in any guise.

This does not mean that you can't or won't fall in love with someone you work with. In this century, the workplace is where many couples meet. But love is not sex and sex is not love. Love in the workplace is fine. Sex is not. And the sex that is inappropriate in the workplace is that which is inappropriate in any setting: sex that will bring harm to others, sex that is obsessive and destructive, sex that is selfish and not thoughtful, sex that is unconscious and uncaring. You get the idea. You know when you engage in sexual misconduct. Sex is a beautiful part of life and we needn't be puritanical about it. Conscious and loving, yes. Mean-spirited and rigid, no. And when you think about it, those parameters define all worthwhile relationships.

So once we begin to adjust our behavior at work and engage in ethical and moral practices, our activities become more enjoyable. The behavior we adopt at work will influence how we behave at home and vice versa, so that our whole life will be marvelously free and interconnected, just as, we begin to notice, the world itself is.

1. For the next week observe your behavior at work without changing anything. But take notes. How often did you cheat your employer out of time by coming in late, leaving early or taking extra time at lunch or coffee breaks? How much time did you spend on personal phone calls or errands? Were you dishonest in any of your business dealings? Was this out of habit or in response to management direction? Keep a list and review it each night, noting what you think and how you feel about your actions.

2. For the second week address some of the behaviors that became evident during the first week and change your approach. Discontinue your bad behavior without putting undue stress on yourself. At the end of each day write about your success and how you are affected emotionally and mentally by this altered behavior. What have you discovered about yourself, your job, your boss? Which was the better week? Which way would you rather live your life?

Congratulations for having the courage to look at your behavior at work (and elsewhere). Congratulations for your willingness to take responsibility for your actions. Congratulations for being honest with yourself and ready to rock your world so that you might learn to live in harmony with the ever-changing circumstances of your life. These are not hollow platitudes and gratuitous kudos. These are sincere offerings. It is not always easy to turn off the automatic pilot that helps us navigate through life, even when we know that operating the controls ourselves will be more rewarding. So give yourself credit. It may seem a rockier road at first, but the views are more breathtaking, the colors more magnificent and the journey more worthwhile.

## The Heart at Work

Daily enjoyment of the time we spend at work is determined by many factors. The work itself is, of course, an important one. But as we've seen, even work that we'd rather not be doing has some value. Even if we're not yet in our final or destined calling, it is important to develop certain facilities, ones that we can carry with us wherever we go. So even if you hate your current job but have decided that you cannot leave it today, concentrate your energies on the suggestions here and each day will become more palatable. And if you love your work, you may grow to love it even more. While the suggestions in this chapter may at first glance seem to have nothing to do with loving your work, they have. Trust me. You won't be disappointed.

Discontinuing our bad behavior on the job is the first step on the road to gaining deep satisfaction in our work. In order to complete this circle and create inner balance and harmony, we must also engage in more positive or good behavior. And we must perform these deeds simply for their own sake without expecting anything from them. That may seem like a tall order, so let's go back for a moment to a question we posed earlier: why being good gets such a bad rap today. And while we're at it, let's add another question/observation to this. Why does the work environment seem to encourage selfish attitudes? Why do so many of us, before deciding to embrace any task, ask ourselves, "What's in it for me?" Spend at least ten minutes now writing about your reactions to these questions and whether or not you believe being good fits into the workplace.

Embedded in our collective cultural psyche is the notion of reward and punishment. If we do something bad, we expect to be punished for it, while doing good will bring rewards of some kind. But our definitions of good and bad often get confused. And we don't want to be seen as too good for fear that we'll be considered weak and taken advantage of. And when we look at successful people, even in our own company, we see that many of them would never be defined as do-gooders. Chances are that they're only out for themselves even as they justify their actions as "good for the company." (Maybe you're one of these people.) And when we get away with bad behavior we rejoice and eventually forget that it's bad. We simply include it in our repertoire with no regrets.

If you have the impulse to turn away from this subject because you don't want a lecture on morals, resist that impulse. Even though we are talking about morals and ethical conduct here, we are not talking about reward and punishment. Certainly we must be aware of the consequences of our behavior; if we embezzle money, we will go to jail. But when choosing a course of action, we must also learn to listen to our internal ethical guide rather than blindly follow an imposed, external set of rules. Each of us knows without having the threat of jail hanging over us that embezzling money is simply wrong. And just as we know this, we also intuitively know what right and good are. We do not need the incentive of reward or the threat of punishment to know the difference between good and bad, right and wrong. Even though we learned the theory of cause and effect earlier, we can never know beforehand exactly what the effects of our actions will be. All we can do is to do the right thing and let the repercussions be whatever they may.

You are capable of both good and bad behavior, and the choice is yours. Sometimes it seems as though we really don't have a choice, that various internal and external pressures, which include the repercussions of our choice, bind us. Some of the pressures that move us are all too real, and while they may seem internal, more often than not they're external: "They'll think I'm crazy," "No one will believe it," "I'll be laughed at, lose my credibility," "My reputation is at stake," "I won't let them win," "I'll be seen as a fool."

Respect and admiration from our peers and superiors are important to most of us. But too often we try to predict how others will perceive our actions. In some cases we may be right. But even if we are, when we attempt to determine our behavior by looking at how others will respond, we lose our footing, stumble and fall, losing ourselves in this process.

When we would rather behave in a bad way we indeed sacrifice a valuable part of ourselves. When we determine our behavior by watching others and decide on the path of least resistance, even if it goes against our moral code, a small piece of our self-respect is lost each time. And when we think that being nice at work is not part of our job description and unnecessary even if it were, because our coworkers do not fall into the category of loved ones, we run the grave risk of becoming coldhearted—a trait that we will certainly carry home with us.

If your work environment is heartless, decide right now that you can change that. If you are in a cutthroat environment and everyone is out for him- or herself alone, decide right now to temper this situation by sharing information with your coworkers. If your workplace is cold and impersonal, decide right now to bring some warmth and personality to it. Intuitively you already know how important it is to be good, to be compassionate, to let your heart lead you, especially at work, given how much time you spend there. Sometimes we need help in the transition between expunging old values and adopting new ones. So if you haven't quite mastered the gentle art of trusting your intuition and you need more convincing, here are some reasons why it's a good idea to bring your heart to work.

It helps you to remember why you're there and what you are really working for.

It reminds you that everyone you encounter throughout your workday also has a heart and is worthy of respect, even if he or she doesn't show it.

It guides you through difficult situations and helps you decide on the right course of action.

It humanizes the workplace without removing it from a professional arena and reminds you that a company is made up of living, breathing human beings. To forget this would be spiritual suicide both for the company and for the individuals in it. Along with your intellect, it will help you appraise the real value of your work and whether or not you belong there.

It will create a sense of balance and help maintain perspective.

It will not interfere with your getting the job done, except where it's spiritually necessary.

It will make you a whole person and will expand all your options.

Even as we begin to carry our heart to work, our values are still bound up with reward and punishment. We may not want to be viewed as too good, but we still want to be given credit. Here's a simple remedy to this: *Do*

WORK FROM THE INSIDE OUT

*good deeds anonymously.* Do them on the sly without anyone finding out. Your ego, your pride and your sense of
fairness will all contribute to your discomfort here. But
do yourself a favor and try it. You will learn a great deal
about yourself, and you will feel good at the end of the
day. Don't choose something so big that the whole
office will be trying to figure out who the perpetrator is.
Keep it small but significant. Every good act need not be
kept a secret, but if you perform one a week, it will be
good for your humility, and your heart will thank you.

---

Here are some other suggestions of how you can
bring your heart to work each day. Try one a week
for a while, see how it feels. Come up with your own
ideas, tailored to suit you and your particular work
environment. There's no reason why you can't have
fun with this. Carrying a smile to work is infectious,
and when you do, it's likely to grow during the day
and be there after work for your friends and family.

1. Help a coworker with a project (without jeopardizing your own job) even if it's "beneath" you or
   not your job.
2. Take out to lunch the person in your department
   that you have the most difficulty working and getting along with. Get to know another aspect of
   this person.
3. If you are in a position to do this, set up a weekly
   or monthly meeting (with coffee and doughnuts)

or other forum in which people in your department will be free to air their questions, concerns, grievances and personal successes without having to worry about repercussions. (If you're not in such a position, either suggest it to someone who is and who'd be open to it or establish such a meeting informally during your lunch hour with interested department members.)

4. If child care issues are a common topic of conversation in the office and if your company doesn't offer any programs or solutions for their employees, rather than continuing to gripe about it, do some research on your own time and present some options to upper management. Even if you don't have kids of your own but have become sensitive to the fact that this is a big issue for others, take on this project. Help to discover a solution. Be proactive in your daily work life. Many corporations are willing to spend money these days on programs that ease the stress of their employees and ultimately contribute to the company's bottom line.

5. Take a few minutes each day to get to know your assistant's or your boss's personal likes and dislikes. And when they're having a bad day, or just for the heck of it, help make their day go a little more smoothly by offering to do something for them or presenting something to them that will put a smile on their face and a little joy in their hearts.

You know better than anyone what your place of work could use to make your heart feel glad. Rather than wait for someone else to take action, do it yourself. You'll feel so much better.

Make a list right now of the things your work environment could use to give it some heart, and do what you can to make it happen. Be open, be realistic and be concerned about all those who share your workspace. You will know what is possible and what you can do. And if nothing else, be courteous and kind to all of your coworkers no matter how they behave. Your behavior is what counts, and your heart can guide you. So take it with you each day, and when you return home it will be fuller and more open.

## The Office Grapevine

Very few of us work in isolation. Even creative artists who spend much of their time working alone deal with a community of people at some point. The community that we work in, which generally consists of individuals much like ourselves, has a huge influence on how we feel about our work. As members, we contribute to or detract from the smooth functioning and spiritual wellness of the larger group. And the health of the big circle determines the welfare of the smaller groups, down to the individuals and back up again—an interdependent, dynamic organism or, if you will, organization. As we saw earlier, our individual actions impact on the larger company and vice versa. What's good or bad for us as workers is then good or bad for the company. The reverse is also true, and it doesn't even matter that the definitions of good and bad sometimes get confused. If we can agree that there is a relationship and powerful symbiosis between the individual and the company, then we can conclude that engaging in right livelihood and taking right action benefit all.

The third leg to this tripod of ethical conduct is right speech. Given that a tripod is an extremely stable structure, it is no coincidence that all three of these components combine to promote a balanced and harmonious life, both for the individual and for the group. This mutuality exists for any group, be it a family, a company, society, your bridge group, a sports team and so on. And the more harmonious the environment, the more satisfied you'll be with your position in the group, your job and the work that you do.

So it's no surprise that what we say and how we say it, as much as what we do not say, will either cause harm or promote good. From the schoolyard to diplomatic circles to intimate relationships, words are used as weapons or as tools of understanding, peace, reconciliation and love. We use (and abuse) our language to communicate most everything. Sometimes we are not even aware of the powerful impact our utterances have on others, though we are usually quite conscious of the impression that their words make on us.

A recent research study to determine the impact of

prayer and meditation on healing elegantly illustrates the power of words and the power of concentration. A group of critically ill patients was randomly divided into two groups. None of the patients was aware of the study beforehand. One group acted as the control group so that results could be measured. The members of the second group were the lucky ones. Their recovery was prayed for and meditated on by a third group of healthy individuals from varied religious and secular organizations. Researchers determined that the significant improvements in the health and well-being of the second group were too great to be attributed to mere chance. So prayer (words offered up to a higher power) and deep, concentrated meditation influenced the physical health of the subjects. Some may say that it was the aspect of prayer and not the words themselves that promoted the healing. I would argue here that the prayers fell into the category of right speech. There was no fear, anger or ego involved. It was a situation of stranger praying for stranger, so all of the usual petty and selfish motives that we sometimes have when we ask for the recovery of a loved one were absent. It was pure and simple speech, offered with good intention and then let go. There were no expectations, no attachment to results, no delusions or illusions, just pure intention, pure prayer—right speech. And the meditation fell into the category of right effort, which will be covered in the next step.

Were you ever admonished with "If you cannot say something good, say nothing at all"? Perhaps you bristle at the suggestion. If so, you might want to investigate your reaction. By now you're practiced in writing about your feelings, so if something has been stirred up, write about it now. And then let's look a little more closely at right and wrong, good and bad speech, and how it affects your daily work life.

You may not have a literal water cooler in your workplace, but chances are you have some version of it where people gossip. Perhaps such "information" gets disseminated in the lunchroom or via e-mail. However or wherever such idle talk is conducted, it usually falls into the category of wrong speech. It is useless, distracting, mostly foolish and more often than not expressed at someone's expense. If you participate in such frivolous conversation, you end up suffering for it. Such idle talk usually has no basis in truth. How can it benefit anyone, let alone foster spiritual wholeness? Ask yourself these questions and review in your mind and then on paper your recent activity in the matter of idle gossip and lies.

---

1. Review the past week at work. Recall the times you listened to gossip and the times you participated in it yourself. Write about the circumstances (or choose one occasion and concentrate your attention on just that one). Write about your feelings at the time and your feelings after, how it affected your performance that day (were you distracted, amused, upset) and your feelings about it now at a distance.

2. Then write about a lie you told, a lie you supported or a lie you denied. This could be something big or small. The magnitude is irrelevant, so maybe it'd be best to start with something small: "The bus was late," "I'm sick today," "I sent it already," "I was never told." Write about how easy or difficult it was to tell such a lie, how accustomed you are to it or not, how it made you feel, and what the repercussions were, if any.

---

Have you ever had a boss who managed through intimidation, who used strong, abusive language to control his or her subordinates? Have you ever done this yourself? Before we reflexively judge someone, let's conjure up some of the compassion we've been learning about. First, how do you feel when someone speaks harshly to you? And are you always aware of your own rude behavior? Sometimes frustration, anger, insecurity or just plain habit causes us to lash out at whomever we can—our boss, our assistants, our children, the bus driver, even ourselves. Understanding such abuse and generating some compassion toward the abuser (even when it's yourself) does not lead us to condone or tolerate such excessive behavior. It simply heightens our awareness and carries us toward knowing exactly how to behave when in the midst. And let's not forget that being around such vitriol is unpleasant and destructive. Never does it motivate (except maybe through fear, but then that creates its own backlash). Never does it promote harmony. And never does it create anything resembling positive growth—for the company or for the individuals involved. So the only solution is to discontinue your own behavior and not react to the behavior of others.

---

Review the past work week and without judgment identify and write about those occasions when rude and abusive language was used. Write about the specifics. Write about your feelings before, during, after and right now. Then write about what could have made it different. What could you have done to defuse the negative atmosphere without enabling anyone? What will you do next time?

---

The best antidote to lies, gossip and harsh language is to engage in noble silence. Say nothing. Don't judge. Don't criticize. Don't try to make it better with words. Simply be silent. Each time you sense a lie coming, say nothing. When you find yourself with others who are in the middle of a gossip session, do not participate, and without calling attention to yourself, walk away or calmly change the subject. Do not react in any way to rude, impolite, harsh or abusive language, and do not engage in it yourself. Just maintain detached silence. If it's a situation at work where a response is expected, ask for some time and then excuse yourself for a short while.

You will be pleasantly surprised how powerful and disarming such silence can be.

Once you become familiar and comfortable with this noble silence and begin abstaining from harmful speech, speaking the truth will come naturally. Without becoming self-righteous, you will no longer care to gossip. Honesty and polite verbal exchange will become second nature. Others will notice. You will feel better each day. Your attention will be focused on important matters, and somehow you will stop hating your boss, your office, your job or whatever it was that created animosity and general dissatisfaction in the first place. You will like yourself more. You will be more tolerant of others. And that will make your daily chores more enjoyable.

Imagine that!

## Office Politics

Even if we love our work, we often end up hating our job. And no matter how many companies we work for, how often we move from one job to the next, sometimes we just cannot find a comfortable niche. We resign ourselves to being miserable and console ourselves with the fact that we still like our work. I've known too many people who have ended up this way.

Getting along with the people at work is a significant factor in job satisfaction. There is more to a job than just doing the job. Fortunately or not, appearances and playing up to the boss are at times almost more important than productivity. So it isn't just our skill at getting the job done that the company considers when it decides whom to hire and whom to keep. (Today, with the marketplace changing and people moving from one company to another more frequently and more often, businesses now find themselves offering more fringe benefits than ever before in order to lure good workers and keep them happy for the long term. But this is the other side of the coin. For now, let's keep our focus on our side and look at what it is that we must do to be happy, not at what we can get.)

After a rocky professional beginning and a number of jobs that just didn't suit him, Eric found himself in a sales position in which he thrived. He loved the product, the customers and the challenges of his job. More than once he was named salesperson of the year. Eric was a self-motivator who didn't need a boss to give him direction or encouragement. His independent spirit was well suited to the loose structure. He got along well with his superiors and his coworkers. Then, as is inevitable, things began to change. The company was sold, upper management was realigned, and the priorities of the organization shifted. Eric's boss, formerly a hands-off manager, became, from Eric's perspective, intrusive, wanting to be informed in detail about Eric's business. Pressure from above was felt by all those below, and Eric hated it and initially refused to change the way he did things, stubbornly holding on to the notion that he knew how to run his business and didn't need anyone, even his boss, interfering. Rather than keeping noble silence, he sat most days in stony silence, communicating only what he felt was important. One day his boss sat him down to inform him that his behavior was unacceptable. Eric had already begun to dread going to work, and this clinched it for him. What his boss then said to him, though not very professional, summed up the issue. He told Eric that if he didn't begin to "suck up" to management, his job was in jeopardy.

Stunned and angry, Eric could hardly believe what he had heard. And though the phrase isn't an elegant one, it clearly elucidated the problem. Luckily Eric was no dummy, so he knew that moving to another company was not the solution. He knew he had to investigate his contribution to the predicament. And then he simply started to communicate better and more often. Furthermore, he did it without resentment. With grace and professionalism he kept his boss informed about the details of his job and his customers. His boss was happy because he then had things to report to his own boss. With this simple solution to what had seemed like a no-win quandary, Eric didn't feel compromised. He did, however, congratulate himself for learning how to play the game. And sometimes, even if it seems as though it has nothing to do with our job performance, we must play the game of office politics. Mostly it's just knowing how to get along with others and giving our superiors what they ask for, not what we think they need.

There is in some workplaces an ugly side to office politics that we should avoid. The rumor mill, backbiting in the name of ambition, slanderous remarks intended to impugn someone's reputation—all of these create mistrust and disharmony. Personal agendas mixed with aggressive speech never come to any good. So even though office politics too often seems to hold a negative connotation, it is only our approach to it and the words we choose to use that determine the outcome.

Right speech, honesty and personal integrity are what is needed in all group situations. If you can say good things or keep noble silence, then your job in this area is done. At that point you are free to express yourself creatively and take responsibility for the level of satisfaction you enjoy from your work. No one else is responsible for the words you choose to say. So choose wisely, and that third leg of ethical conduct will strengthen your moral character and bring balance and harmony to your life.

*Those who know don't talk.*
*Those who talk don't know.*

*Block the openings;*
*Close the doors;*
*Soften the glare;*
*Settle your dust;*
*Blunt your edges;*
*Untangle your knots.*
*This is called mysterious oneness.*

*Therefore, it introduces you to the Way.*
*You cannot get close to it nor remove yourself from it.*
*You cannot benefit nor harm it.*
*You cannot honor nor debase it.*
*This is why it's the noblest thing in the world.*

TAO TE CHING (#56)

## The Fifth Step
# DISCIPLINED
# ATTENTION

■

In this fifth step we will learn how to further cultivate our awareness, our moment-to-moment alertness. We have already noticed how our tendency to brood about the past or worry about the future contributes to our unhappiness in the present. And we have either experienced for ourselves or have at least recognized how important it is to be present in the here and now and accept whatever our life offers us. But we also know that there can be a huge gap between accepting the possibility of a happy existence and living in the reality of one, just as in theory we can firmly believe that it's possible to make a decision and change in an instant from a dissatisfied state to a satisfied one but in reality we usually have to work hard for such grace.

This step is about developing mental discipline and paying attention to our states of mind, our concepts of reality—where we are and what it is we're actually doing. It is about being courageous enough to closely observe our own behavior, our moods, how we think about work and how we react to it. It is about bearing witness to our life so that we might reach an understanding about it.

In our search for a fulfilling work life we may decide that we need further training before we can realize our goals. Our course depends on our career choice. We might return to school to educate ourselves and accumulate the appropriate knowledge, or we might need to train our bodies or hone our artistic skills. And on-the-job-training further adds to our expertise once we are ensconced in the work we've chosen. If we've chosen badly or realize our mistake after investing time and money, we sometimes feel trapped and are unable or unwilling to move. Though it may call for some sacrifice and much patience, changing careers when we know what we want to do is relatively easy. What's not so easy is finding happiness in our work when we're uncertain about what we want to do, when we don't have a yearning passion to do a particular thing, when no work of any kind appeals to us, when we've tried everything and can't find a match or when we are doing the work we love but are still discontent.

No matter our level of education or training, each of us knows how necessary learning is. When we think of such skills as reading and writing, we see how once we acquire them we often take them for granted. But no one learns to read and write without some training and discipline. In step five you will learn how to discipline your mind and cultivate awareness so that you can achieve a happy and contented work life. Disciplining ourselves so that we can be happy might seem oxymoronic. And you might say, "Being happy is my inalienable right, so why must I work at it?" To this I would say that we always have a deeper appreciation for something we've worked at, so why not work at gaining happiness? And while we're at it, why not reverse our opinion of work and begin to delight in the "work" of happiness? In step five you will be asked to look at things in a completely new way. Why not begin right now by seeing the discipline, the work of this step, as a good thing rather than a necessary evil, as a joy rather than a burden, as a fun adventure rather than a dreary chore? Adopting this new attitude will serve you well as you move through this step. Open your mind. Unclench your heart. All of this is for you, for your happiness, for your spiritual well-being and for your joyous work life.

*Act without doing,*
*work without effort.*
*Find flavor in the unsavory.*

*See the small as large*
*and the few as many.*
*Be kind to those who foster resentment.*

*Attend to the difficult while it is still easy;*
*do the big things by beginning with the small.*
*Difficult things start out as easy;*
*big things begin as small.*

*The wise person never strives for success,*
*therefore she achieves it.*
*One who makes easy promises is not to be trusted.*
*One who sees everything as easy will experience much*
*difficulty.*
*The wise person knows that some things are difficult,*
*and she embraces them;*
*therefore she is free of all difficulties.*

TAO TE CHING (#63)

# Making the Effort

Being employed in the right field, with the right company and in the right environment are all factors that contribute to our work satisfaction. But these alone are not enough to guarantee a happy work life. When we find the right job we tend to think that our work is done and from then on it will be smooth sailing. But there is more to do—on ourselves, on our mind and on our spirit. We must discipline and train our mind in ways that at first glance seem to have nothing to do with work. This is where we struggle to learn a new language, a new vocabulary. If you truly want freedom and happiness, a lazy approach will not take you there. So make the effort and soon enough it will become second nature. Though the learning curve is steep, the rewards are well worth the climb.

Our state of mind on any given day determines whether that day will be a good one or a bad one, enjoyable or painful. When we are upset and in mental turmoil our outlook will be negatively slanted, and no matter how good the day we often can't see anything good in it. The reverse is true as well, as on some days nothing can shake us from feeling centered and strong no matter how bad it is. Usually we allow our states of mind to carry the day, not realizing how responsible we are for them. But there is something we can do to change this haphazard pattern. We can exercise our will and make the effort to regulate our state of mind.

As you approach this part of the step, keep in mind the interrelatedness of everything. You needn't master this part before moving on to the next. You may never perfect any of this. This is about progress, about life, about challenge and making the effort.

There are four ways to practice right effort so that you can live in a state of equanimity and joy.

1. *Do not allow morally harmful states of mind to arise or negative behavior patterns to become established.* You have more control over your mind, and particularly over your behavior, than you think. And you know, especially if you paid attention and spent time on step four, what your moral boundaries are. When you pay attention you become attuned to the behavior, situations and people that ignite unwholesome states of mind, which too often lead to questionable behavior. Make the effort to avoid such situations. And when you consciously decide to

control your state of mind and reside in a wholesome place, then an internal shift begins to take place and your world becomes more sharply focused.

This is a rather easy effort to make, since all you have to do is prevent negative patterns from establishing themselves. There is an old Zen saying that perfectly summarizes your challenge here: "The occurrence of an evil thought is a malady; not to continue it is the remedy."

When first starting on this new path of behavior, we will continue to think and behave in the usual ways. But as we sharpen our mental acuity we will notice troublesome thoughts or negative impulses as soon as they occur. Then we just acknowledge the thought or behavior, without judgment, and simply let it go. We do not follow it, grasp it or hold on to it for any reason.

There will be many challenges here as others get away with or are rewarded for despicable behavior. Our old way of thinking might tell us, "It's not so bad. They're not bad people, and I just want to fit in. Maybe doing what they do will help." Remind yourself that this is your ego talking. Be careful here of the tendency to place yourself above others on the moral high ground. Self-righteousness is one of the states of mind to be avoided, as is judgment of others. Recognize these tendencies before they become established.

2. *Work to dispel the morally compromising, ambiguous or destructive states of mind that already exist within you and the behaviors that accompany them.* You might want to make a mental checklist of where you stand on certain ethical

and moral issues. Review your habitual ways of thinking, your habitual patterns of behavior: the ones that are destructive to you or others, the ones that go against your sense of right and wrong but which you feel you have no control over.

Before we can truly love what we do and do what we love it is necessary to develop some self-awareness. This comes when we take the time and make the effort to be still, to pay attention, to really investigate our inner workings and their outer manifestations. Identify old habits that compromise your peace of mind and work on tearing them down brick by brick. Maybe you have a habit of always being late to work (if so, you most likely are never on time for anyone, so the opportunity to work on this will come up often), you make excuses to leave early or you take extra time at lunch. Without calling too much attention to yourself, start being on time. Investigate your old attitudes toward lateness and get to the source so that you can truly expel the habitual pattern. Or maybe you are the gossipmonger at work, the one always in a bad mood, the tyrant or taskmaster. You know what needs to go. Make the effort. Do some housecleaning. Get rid of the old, make room for the new.

3. *Create new and wholesome states of mind and establish new behavior patterns that support your emerging outlook.* When we begin to refrain from destructive thoughts and actions and discontinue bad habits, we free up some space to begin developing new habits, positive states of mind and patterns of behavior that promote rather than restrict

our progress toward a free and happy existence. There are six virtues that can be practiced to help encourage change and enhance your everyday work life.

*Generosity.* Be unstinting with yourself, your time, energy and expertise. Help others where you can. Give away what you have, and even more will come back to you. Be kind and generous with your spirit.

*Morality.* Practice proper behavior in the office (and, it goes without saying, also with friends, family and even strangers). Do not lie, steal, cheat or engage in illicit sexual conduct.

*Patience.* Be tolerant of others and forgive them their shortcomings. Practice acceptance of things as they are and the sometimes mysterious workings of your boss or organization. Allow things to unfold naturally without attempting to force an outcome.

*Perseverance.* Be diligent, enthusiastic and determined in all that you do.

*Concentration.* Pay attention to each moment, each task and each encounter of each day. Meditate on your contribution and be mindful that you are but one part of a larger whole.

*Intuitiveness.* Trust your instincts. Do not rely on intellectual knowledge alone. Be understanding and centered in the wisdom gained as a result of practicing and living in these steps.

4. *Further develop and perfect your existing positive and wholesome states of mind and patterns of behavior.* Keep in mind that a complete and total transformation is not necessary here, even though it may sometimes seem that way. Much that you do is good and pure. As you get to know yourself better you will recognize your virtues and realize that you're not a lost cause. In fact, you are pretty special in a multitude of ways. Nurture these qualities. Let the world see them. It is not boasting. It is simply exposing the utter truth and beauty of your being.

## Eyes Wide Open

If there is but one thing that you get from this book, let it be the concept and then the practice of mindfulness. If you actually practice this in every moment, then all the pieces will fall into place, life will make sense and nothing will be left to "do." But because this sort of moment-to-moment awareness does not come naturally, it is necessary to work at it, to make the effort, to establish a discipline and to incorporate a method of mindfulness in all that you do.

There are four ways in which to practice mindfulness: (1) with the body, (2) with feelings and sensations, (3) with the mind and (4) with ideas and thoughts. Let's begin our mindfulness exploration with the body.

No one can argue with the fact that in whatever we do, wherever we go, our bodies come along. Sometimes they are a bother—when we get sick or hurt, for instance. And sometimes we become unduly preoccupied with them—either compulsively working out or constantly dieting, for example. But how many of us can say that we are truly connected to our bodies? And once we pose that question, how many of us wonder why it even matters, especially when all we're trying to do is figure out how we might be happier with our work life. What does the one have to do with the other? The answer is simple: everything. When we are in our bodies rather than just in our heads, then all things become possible. We become grounded, highly aware of all that is going on in and around us and more capable of making our way through it comfortably and happily. Here are some of the practical reasons for developing body mindfulness:

> It eliminates stress.
> It lowers blood pressure and anxiety.
> It improves physical health.
> It assuages fatigue.
> It restores normal sleep patterns.

All of the above benefits serve to:

> Increase productivity and efficiency.
> Enhance job performance and satisfaction.
> Improve relationships at work with supervisors
> and coworkers.
> Heighten the ability to focus on the task at hand.

Broaden comprehension, perception and memory skills, leading to more creative thinking.

There are two main ways to practice body mindfulness. The first is with the breath. Just by sitting quietly with all your attention focused on your breath, wonderful things can happen. They may not happen while you're doing this breathing practice, and at first you may not make the connection between the practice and its effects, but eventually, when your awareness is honed, you will know that the peace of mind you enjoy, the calm with which you handle previously disturbing situations and the subtle, deep joy you feel at the strangest moments can only be attributed to this breath-attention practice. The breathing exercises at the end of step three (pages 132–137) are a good place to start. If you set aside just ten minutes at the beginning of your day and ten minutes at the end of your day to just sit and breathe, you will be amazed by the results. Add to this as you go along and as you begin to experience the effects. Some more suggestions of how, when and where to just breathe:

1. Take five or ten minutes out of your lunch or coffee break, find a spot where you can be relatively undisturbed and focus on your breath.
2. Whenever you feel your fear, anxiety, anger or frustration levels rising, take a five- or even two-minute time-out. Close your eyes and bring all your attention into your body. Relax your shoulders, scan your body for tension, breathe into it

and exhale it away. Soften your grip on whatever you're holding on to. Breathe into your belly and out through your toes.

3. Gradually increase the time you spend at the beginning and end of your day on this breath work, working your way up to the technique described in step three, breath exercise #5, page 137.

When you first begin to breathe mindfully and draw your attention into your body, you will quite naturally do it with your eyes closed. But once your breathing slows down and your attention shifts, it is best to open your eyes and concentrate that way. If you keep your eyes closed, you will tend to daydream or fall asleep, neither of which is the intention here. With open eyes you can really be in *this* moment, right now. At first your mind will wander, your attention will be distracted. The slightest noise will disturb you, and thoughts will insinuate themselves and try to draw you away. Do not be seduced by any of this. Simply continue breathing. When you become aware that your attention has strayed, return to the count of one on the next exhale. Open your eyes. Focus on nothing but your breath. At some point you will experience a moment, maybe only a split second, of deep, full and total concentration. You will be aware of nothing but your breath. The sound that was bothering you a moment before will no longer exist for you. No thoughts intrude. You feel joy, happiness and maybe even bliss. You want to hold on to this feeling. You cannot. The next moment you are self-conscious

WORK FROM THE INSIDE OUT

once again. But if you keep it up, if you practice this breath-attention exercise with diligence and patience, those moments of total, joyful concentration will expand and you will lose yourself in mindful breathing, which in turn will increase your ability to concentrate, both during your breathing exercises and at other times during the day. This unselfconscious mode of being will be the rule rather than the exception, and you will be fully awake, aware and attentive to even the smallest details of your life. And this practice will teach you in a very tangible way that if you are self-conscious, you cannot concentrate on anything well.

The second way to practice body mindfulness is to be aware of what you do and say. Pay close attention to the task at hand. Concentrate on what you are doing now, not on what you did or didn't do yesterday or on what you need to do tomorrow. Allowing the distractions around you (and there often can be many) to take you away from the project at hand only serves to delay completion, raise anxiety and compromise the quality and enjoyment of your work. Your work can become so routinely automatic that you go through the motions without really being there. And if you're not really there, you cannot expect to enjoy your work or gain any satisfaction from it. Let's look at one common daily activity that anyone can relate to and learn from: eating. This is something we all do at least once every day. But how often do you do it mindlessly, on the run or along with one or two other things? When was the last time you sat down to a meal and really paid attention to what you were eating?

At your very next meal turn off the TV, close the book or newspaper and concentrate on the food in front of you. It's okay to dine with others and talk, but pay close attention to the meal itself. Be aware of each bite. Concentrate on the flavor sensations. Just eat. Lose your self in the process. Notice the colors and textures of the food. Chew mindfully. If the food is especially good, be careful not to rush to the next bite. If you eat this way, chances are you won't overeat, chances are you'll become aware of old eating habits that need to change. And you'll gain a new appreciation for why you eat.

Next, take this mindful behavior to work with you. If your job is or has become routine, start by varying, if only slightly, the routine. Doing this will help you to pay closer attention. Approach each task as if for the first time. If we ever tire or get bored with eating, we usually know it's about us and not the food. Same with work. Same with any activity. And all it takes to renew the enjoyment is a little concentrated effort. If it's a food you don't like, stop eating it. If it's a job you truly hate doing (and once you really pay attention you will know for sure), then maybe it's time to change jobs. Often-times, though, we discover that it's not the job, it's us. And when we really pay attention to what we're doing and lose ourselves in the work, then the satisfaction, the enjoyment of doing it, escalates.

If your job is varied, hectic and unpredictable, it is still possible to be mindful. Even if demands are being made of you from many different quarters, you can still do only one thing at a time. So as you do that one thing concentrate completely on it. All the other things will be waiting for you when you're done or ready for them. Tackle each task mindfully and not only will you become more productive, you will begin to enjoy it all more. Sometimes you just can't do it all. When you concentrate mindfully on each thing you do, it may become apparent that more is expected of you than is possible to accomplish. Then it might be time to speak up. Say something. Be mindful of what you say, how you say it and to whom you say it. And remember, if you cannot accomplish all that you've been given, you will know what action to take next if you're mindful and honest with yourself. You will know if your boss's demands are unrealistic or if you've allowed yourself to take on more than you can handle. You will know if you're up to the task or if no one could possibly do it all. Paying attention and being mindful bring clarity and deeper satisfaction.


Glenn loved his job, and he was good at it. It seemed to him and everyone else that he was a born salesperson. His superiors loved him, and his clients trusted him. He made money for all and was well compensated for his efforts. Glenn was also involved with a spiritual community and committed to a meditation practice that helped him carry mindfulness to work with him. This contributed greatly to his love of work and to his high level of performance. His superiors observed that he was more productive and apparently less stressed than his coworkers, and they began adding to Glenn's workload. They gave him more accounts and more products to sell. Glenn continued to perform well, but the added burden began to take its toll. His attitude toward the job took on a slightly negative cast, and there were days when he didn't look forward to going to work. Although Glenn was able to absorb himself in his work once he was there, he wasn't willing to admit that he had been given more work than he could handle, because he did handle it. So he couldn't bring himself to ask his superiors to lighten his workload. In his mind, his eroding personal satisfaction didn't justify it. He continued on until he became miserable enough to accept another job that would allow him to resume a healthy lifestyle. He liked his job, his company and the people he worked with and didn't really want to leave, but he felt that he had no choice. And his company was sad to see him go but did nothing to keep him. Sometime later Glenn heard that two people had been hired to replace him and cover his territory. This did not surprise him. It did make him all the more aware that he still needed to learn how to speak up for himself, trust his instincts and not let anyone take advantage of him simply because he enjoyed his work and had learned how to handle the stress of the job.

What prevented Glenn from speaking up for himself, other than pride, was fear: fear of losing his job, fear of what others would think of him, fear of inadequacy, fear of whatever. Just plain fear. Speaking of which, the two biggest fears that human beings have are fear of dying and fear of public speaking, with the latter sometimes being the greater. This fear of public speaking relates both to the body mindfulness we've been talking about and to the workplace, since so many jobs require public speaking of some sort, such as in presentations to clients or coworkers, departmental or company-wide business meetings and training sessions. This fear might be what's keeping you back from pursuing your dream job. Perhaps it keeps you anonymous within your own company and interferes with advancement. The way to overcome this fear is with mindfulness and practice.

If you become practiced at being mindful in all that you do—each task at work, every encounter with a coworker, eating, sleeping, rising, walking, talking, bathing and so on—then speaking to a group will just be an extension of this honed skill. If your self becomes conscious of the fact that you're speaking to a group—"Oh my, here I am standing up here and addressing these people"—then you will falter and the fear will take over. Instead it is important to get lost in the act of speaking. Just speak. Lose your self. Unselfconsciously devote your attention to what you're saying. Maintain mindfulness. And then public speaking (or going in to talk to the boss, voicing your opinion at work or standing up for yourself) will be as easy as eating and maybe even as enjoyable. In your breathing exercises you learn to keep bringing your attention back to your breath when thoughts arise or an itch of some sort wants your attention. It is just the same with activity mindfulness. Keep bringing your attention back to the task, to whatever it is you're saying, doing or listening to. Let your breath be your guide. And before you know it, that blissful state of total absorption will take over and you will be *just* doing, *just* speaking, *just* listening, *just* being. Just that. Just.

## Don't Worry About Your Worries

Throughout this book I've referred again and again to the state of dissatisfaction and how we can change it. And perhaps what drew you to this book was your own unhappiness with work and a desire to do something about it. We all have such unwanted feelings at one time or another. But rather than let them drag us around, rather than have the feelings color our view of every-thing—even the feelings themselves—we can learn another way, a mindful way, to look at and approach them: *view each feeling as a feeling, not as "my feeling."*

Early in this process we learned about the false idea of self that we all have. With this in mind, take your self out of the picture as you mindfully explore your feelings and notice how you tend to compound each feeling with yet more feelings. When feeling unhappy, for example, you may become unhappy about being unhappy. You may even add depression and sorrow to the mix. We worry about our worries. And then we become sad or hurt about being worried.

The first thing you must do as you practice feeling mindfulness is not to be dissatisfied with your dissatisfaction. Feel the feeling but be objective about it at the same time. Rather than seeing it as "my feeling," see it simply as *a* feeling. Investigate this feeling. Look for its cause. Watch its trajectory. Notice how it arises and when it ends. Be the objective witness to each feeling. Pay attention. See how it comes and how it goes.

View your mind in this same way. Be the objective scientist. Be aware whenever your mind is overcome with anger or love. Notice when it becomes attached to a feeling, an idea, an emotion. And then notice what happens when you detach from it. Notice the change, the freedom. As you begin to practice these mindful excursions, some old habits and old voices may try to assert themselves. It is a powerful experience to look honestly at yourself, to really see what goes on. And it's not always easy to look. Judgment and criticism want to have their say. But with all types of mindfulness remember that you are observing, examining and listening carefully. Nothing else.

The paradox of being mindful of and detached from our feelings and the workings of our mind is that we begin to take things less personally while at the same time becoming more engaged in our life.


Virginia has been in the same field for over twenty years. Work has been the main focus in her life, and it has given her a sense of identity and purpose. Virginia presented herself to the outside world, to her friends and to her family as a successful businesswoman who loved her job. And the demands of her job often claimed priority over everything else. No one questioned it. At least she was happy with her work, as so many others around her weren't. She was seen as being engaged and involved. Nothing wrong with that.

The first time Virginia was fired everyone who knew her was shocked, including herself. There was blame, finger-pointing, rationalizations and excuses, then anger and self-recriminations. Virginia took it personally, sought out psychological counseling and eventually recovered and moved on to the next job, which she threw herself into wholeheartedly, not wanting to repeat the experience of being fired. She worked harder and longer than her coworkers, but her personal satisfaction began to wane. She wouldn't let up on herself, though. To outsiders Virginia was just being Virginia—absorbed in and even consumed with her job.

When she got fired a second time there was a handy excuse of merger mania and downsizing. It eased the pain somewhat, but again Virginia took it personally and made a vow to herself that it absolutely would never happen again. She would do everything in her power to prevent it. The next job didn't come so quickly, though. The hiatus, which lasted a year, eroded Virginia's self-confidence and self-esteem. Worry took over, and she didn't enjoy even one day of this break. The relief she experienced when she was offered a job was palpable. It was a good job, high-paying, responsible and demanding. Virginia felt up to it but never forgot her vow. So once more she threw herself into her work.

The toll of the two firings, the yearlong hiatus and the abundant energy she had invested in her work life began to show. Again Virginia worked long hours, "self-lessly" giving to the job. She convinced herself and others that it was necessary in order to get the job done. Stress began to get the better of her. Though she was in therapy and seemingly aware of her self, fear and anxiety were now constant companions.

When Virginia's immediate supervisor was replaced, Virginia knew there would be trouble. She and the new supervisor just did not get along. Virginia was let go once again. This time, though, it was a relief. Her new boss did for her what she couldn't do for herself. And because she had fared just fine before he arrived on the scene she could easily, without guilt, point the finger at him and say it was his fault. He just didn't like her and was in a position to get rid of her. It wasn't her fault. This time she didn't take it personally. It was a personality conflict, and her personality was not the issue.

There is a lot in Virginia's work life that we could analyze: her apparent addiction to work, the fear that motivated her, the clinging and the denial, for starters. But since we're on the subject of mindfulness, let's focus on that and on Virginia's tendency to take the events of her life personally or not.

Virginia liked her work well enough (she herself has admitted this) and she was quite competent (her longevity in the field and the position she rose to testify to this). But there was something in Virginia's makeup that caused her to worry about job security. If she had been practicing mindfulness, she would have been able to look at the worry, come to an understanding of why she had it, let it be and move on. Instead the worry took over and dictated her behavior. She hung on to her job for dear life, thinking that would bring security. But the holding on made her tense and rigid. She took everything too seriously and very personally. When she was fired her worst fears were realized. She did take some action to ease her pain by seeking counseling, and it did help her cope, but it just wasn't enough. If she had been practicing mindfulness, she might have seen how her grasping and holding on negatively affected her productivity and her ability to work well with others. She did take charge at work, and part of her responsibilities included listening to others. But she always had her mind made up before anyone else had a chance to contribute. She thought she listened, but her own voice was all she heard. This self-absorption became evident to others even though there was no outward and obvious behavioral sign. Many of the long hours Virginia put in were used to cover herself so that she would be blamed for nothing. Even she never realized what she was doing because her fear and denial were so robust.

By the time the third firing took place, Virginia had boxed herself in so tightly that she was a wound-up ball of tension and worry. She had lost herself somewhere along the way and didn't even know what she felt. All she knew was that she couldn't take the blame, she couldn't look at her part in all of it, because for sure she would explode if she did. She even congratulated herself for saying that being fired had nothing to do with her. She was okay with it. It was her boss's problem, not hers. She did everything right. And she would survive. She claimed that she didn't take it personally, but she took it very personally indeed.

If Virginia never learns how to practice mindfulness, she will of course still survive. She'll get another job, she'll perform well and she'll once again have the sense of security supplied by a regular paycheck and a sixty-hour workweek. Virginia will most likely never be truly happy in her work if she continues on this course. But it's not too late for her to change. The first thing she can do is deal with the anger and hurt about being fired that she continues to harbor. And rather than justify the anger and hurt, or point the finger elsewhere to avoid facing some truth, what she can do is mindfully and objectively observe the hurt and anger, exploring her feelings and how her mind handles them, seeing where the feelings go without becoming attached to them. Then little by little, step by step, she can go back and mindfully look at her recent behavior at work. There's no need to go too far back, as chances are she estab-lished a pattern early on that became habitual, so her later behavior most certainly mirrors her early behavior. It's only important to look at the pattern and then change it. Going forward, Virginia can then be diligent about observing her behavior, her feelings and her mind as she brings a mindful attitude to everything—the job search, the eventual new job, the worry that will try to reassert itself, the fear, the joy. Though at first Virginia will feel raw and uncertain, she will also feel very much alive and engaged in her life, more so than ever before. Though her habitual patterns will try to take hold, if she's mindful, they will eventually disappear and be replaced with attentive moment-by-moment awareness and aliveness. She may notice her priorities shifting. She may see the need to work sixty hours a week recede. She may have time on her hands to spend with herself, her friends and her family. She may get to know herself in a new way, and though more self-aware, she will not take things so personally anymore. She might even decide that she enjoys her work more than she thought she did. She will see nothing wrong with having a good time doing something she loves. Her new coworkers will admire and like rather than fear her. It is her choice. It is her life. But if she engages in right effort and practices mindfulness, she will never be the same again. She will be richer and more satisfied in all ways. If you were Virginia, what would you do?

## You Are (and Aren't) Your Work

Whenever we take the changing circumstances of our life too personally, we lose perspective on what is happening, on how we feel or what we think. Mindfulness prepares us for change and increases understanding. If Virginia, whom we met in the last section, had developed mindful behavior, she wouldn't have taken the events of her life so personally, which would have enabled her to see her part in those events. Taking things personally prevents us from taking responsibility even if we blame ourselves.

The fourth way we can develop and practice mindfulness is to meditate on or contemplate issues and ideas. For example, if you find an idea difficult to understand, don't turn your back on it. Instead meditate on it. Just sit with the idea, contemplate its meaning and see what thoughts arise.

You can take this mindful approach to work and use it to come to a clearer understanding of the issues that confuse or irritate you. In fact, if you follow the suggestions in this book, you will constantly be practicing this mindful exercise. You will know yourself vis-à-vis work a lot better after your first run through this process. And more the second time. And even more the third. You will never be done with it, as it is ongoing. And as you proceed on this journey you will be presented with a multitude of opportunities to practice mindfulness.

There are five hindrances that to some degree we all confront along the way. They obstruct our path, cloud our thinking and interrupt our smooth progress. They are:

1. Craving
2. Ill will
3. Laziness
4. Restlessness
5. Doubt

You can wait for them to show up or you can take the time now to better understand how they operate in your life. Meditate on these five points and how they insinuate themselves into your life. You need do nothing else now but contemplate them. You might desire to change, or you might notice your attachment and your fear of letting go. Just watch. Simply become aware of the roles they play in your life. Once you have done this, you will be more willing and able to let go.

It is also a good idea, for balance, to meditate on the more positive aspects of life. Review the factors that you deem important for a healthy, happy life and meditate on each one. How and where does it fit in your life? Here are some areas to look at:

1. Mindfulness
2. Ethical conduct
3. Energy or determination
4. Joy
5. Equanimity

There are many more to consider, so come up with your own list.

---

1. Write two lists: one list of all those things that you believe interfere with your spiritual progress and with enjoying a satisfying work life (limit the list to those things you have some control over; it can

include some or all of the five hindrances listed above), and another list of the factors that you believe are important and necessary for a happy and fulfilling life (again, include only those you can influence, and don't worry about whether or not life right now contains these qualities).

2. Spend some time mindfully reviewing these two lists, sharpening your vision and ushering in clarity. Keep coming back to them in concentrated stillness as your understanding grows.

3. Investigate and mindfully concentrate on the occurrence in your life of the following two scenarios:

   a. You define yourself by what you do. You are in and out of work a lawyer or waitress or whatever. Even if you don't like your work or chosen profession, you see yourself as a lawyer or waitress, even as you work hard to deny it. By resisting or embracing the label (it makes no difference which it is) you become it, and by doing that you limit yourself.

   b. Your work defines you; you become your work. You don't think about what you do, you just do it. You lose your self, the label, the title, in the work itself. You become a worker doing the work and then there is no separation between you and the work. It is simply working.

Which of the above scenarios have you experienced? If both, which feels better? If you've never experienced b, the mindfulness activities here will help you to achieve this state of work absorption. If you've only rarely experienced it, you at least know the feeling, so practice mindful attention at work and you will know it more often. Practice mindful attention in all activities, in and out of work. Break down your old habitual patterns of behavior by paying attention to each moment, and you will love whatever task you are engaged in.

## One-Pointedness

There is one discipline that is essential to accomplishing anything you set out to do well, a discipline that will take you through each exercise suggested here, help you cope with the inevitable distractions, allow you to be present in each moment and help you achieve balance as you deal with changing circumstances. In order to achieve some measure of peace you must be familiar with this activity. No honest and intimate relationship can exist without it. Your interpersonal interactions at work run more smoothly if you engage it. Every aspect of your life, large and small, needs it. Even if you haven't yet guessed what it is, it will make perfect sense when you see it. And what is it? Concentration.

Just reading this book takes a certain amount of it. Driving your car, walking across a busy street, shaving, using any sharp instrument—all of these activities demand it. Without even thinking about it, you engage in concentrated effort whenever the occasion calls for it. And if you've done any of the exercises in this book, you've employed it. Imagine what your life would be like if you were in a state of total concentration each moment. You would always know where you left your keys, when you mailed those letters, what you had for lunch. No time would be wasted. Therefore you'd have more of it. There would even be time for daydreaming, an activity that shouldn't be excluded but which you needn't let control you. Whether you are aware of it or not, you waste precious time every day worrying, fretting, yearning. As you build up your concentration muscles, all those things will fade.

The breathing and mindfulness exercises, along with the writing and thinking exercises, have all honed your concentration. Perhaps you've already increased the use of this discipline at work and have experienced some of the benefits or gained insight into your work problem. And perhaps you're willing to develop this skill even further so that peace of mind and true awareness can be yours.

Establishing a practice of sitting meditation at home will accelerate the process of honing your concentration. Sitting meditation is not easy to do. You will be bothered by distractions. And the hindrances that we spoke of earlier (restlessness, doubt, and the like) will present themselves and challenge your commitment. But perseverance will bring rewards.

You will even need some concentration as you approach the following exercises. Think of it as the flour in a loaf of bread. The loaf (the concentration you will develop) cannot exist without the flour (the concentration you bring to these practices). And remember that in order for the flour to become bread it needs to be combined with other ingredients, then kneaded, risen, risen some more, and finally baked. A lot of time and preparation go into the making of one loaf of bread. So don't get discouraged too quickly here. If you invest time and energy into these exercises, your concentration will eventually be "cooked."

---

### CONCENTRATION EXERCISE #1: SITTING STILL NO MATTER WHAT

*Earlier in this process I suggested setting some time aside each day to spend in quiet meditation. If you haven't yet begun doing this, now is the time. As you enter into each meditation period, express your commitment to it by framing it in ritual. Turn down the lights and say a prayer or light a candle. Then prepare your body for sitting still. Arrange yourself comfortably on cushions on the floor or on a straight-backed chair, making sure your spine is erect and you can breathe comfortably. Then sit for ten minutes absolutely still, with only your breath moving your body. Concentrate completely on your breath and count each exhale, slowly and silently. One to five. One to five. And remember to keep your eyes open. If you have an itch, don't scratch it; just keep your concentration on your breath. If you feel muscle pain or a cramp someplace, allow it to be painful for the moment; don't move or try to squirm it away, and keep breathing, keep counting. When thoughts intrude (and they*

WORK FROM THE INSIDE OUT

will), don't continue thinking the thought; just notice that you had it and keep breathing, keep counting. If you lose your place, start over again, at one, on your next exhale. Don't allow this to interfere. Keep concentrating. Your mind will wander. Your body will scream for release. Just keep sitting still, breathing and counting, no matter what. Concentrate. Relax. It's only ten minutes. It's not forever, though it may seem that way. So that you needn't be constantly checking the time, run a blank tape for ten minutes with some gentle sound or soft music recorded at the end of the ten minutes to signal the end. The more you practice this (I suggest at least once every day) the easier it will become. Your mind will quiet down, your body will relax and your concentration will gain strength.

---

## CONCENTRATION EXERCISE #2:
## SPEND A FEW MINUTES WITH A RAISIN

Select one raisin and pick it up between your thumb and index finger. Decide that for the next few minutes the world will consist only of you and that raisin. Before putting it in your mouth (notice the impulse to do so), place it in the palm of your hand. Observe its shape, color and texture. Smell it. Slowly bring it to your lips, touch your tongue to it. Become aware of the different sensations. Once it's in your mouth (take your time getting it there), chew it very slowly. Concentrate on the taste. Do not swallow it. Keep chewing, with all your energy devoted to just chewing. Count the number of times you chew—twenty, thirty, forty, up to one hundred. Let the raisin reduce down to its juices and then slowly swallow it. Savor the taste. When all trace of it is gone, pick up another raisin and repeat this process. Keep bringing your attention back to the raisin. Notice your impatience. Let it go. Concentrate on the raisin alone. Do it a third time, just for good measure.

---

## CONCENTRATION EXERCISE #3:
## THE FIFTH EXHALATION

*Bring yourself to a comfortable seated posture, as in exercise 1. Spend a minute or two breathing slowly and regularly, then begin your breathing meditation. As you exhale, silently say the number of the exhalation for the full length of it (this will help your concentration). On the fifth breath extend your exhalation and release more air out of your lungs than you normally do. Keep letting air out until there is no more. Then inhale and resume counting, starting at one. Again, on the next fifth exhale slowly release all the air, and then some, out of your lungs, keeping your full attention on the exhalation. Continue for the entire ten-minute session, extending each fifth exhalation. End each of these sessions with a minute or two of regular, slow, concentrated breathing.*

---

## CONCENTRATION EXERCISE #4:
## JUST WASHING

*Choose one of your regular daily activities and concentrate your complete attention on every detail as you do it, for the whole period of doing it, or for at least ten minutes. It could be bathing, dressing, washing the dishes, preparing dinner or lifting weights. Pay complete attention as you turn on the water, wet your body, pick up the soap and so on. Be there completely, in each action.*

To do this you might have to silently narrate the exercise: "Now I am washing my legs, washing my thighs, my knees, my shins, my ankles." Keep your attention solely concentrated on each minute detail.

---

## CONCENTRATION EXERCISE #5:
## UP THE ANTE

Extend the time spent on exercise 1 to fifteen and then twenty minutes. Over time you will begin to notice the effects, and not only will it become easier but you will begin to look forward to this time each day. Challenge yourself every so often and go for thirty or even forty minutes. You can do way more than your mind tells you you can. If you have a friend to do this with, it will make it easier. You can support and encourage each other. When you feel like giving up on yourself you might choose to continue for your friend's sake. And if you can't find a suitable companion for these exercises, dedicate each one to someone you love. Do it for him or her. Both of you will reap the benefits.

---

## CONCENTRATION EXERCISE #6:
## TAKE IT TO WORK

Begin to engage throughout the workday the concentration skills you are developing. Each time you become distracted from the task at hand (by certain feelings, by a coworker wishing to gossip, by an unnecessary personal phone call, by your disdain for the chore in front of you and the desire to procrastinate) pull yourself back to this moment with your breath and focus directly and exclusively on the project in front of you. Approach it as if *you were doing it for the very first time. And then just do it. Just for the sake of doing it. Do not think about why you're doing it. Just do it. Do not look forward to its completion. Just be there with it as you do it. Bring this steady concentration to the work you are doing even when you're not distracted.*

---

When you practice still, silent meditation in a clear, concentrated manner, you can look forward to progressing in a delightful way. This time-tested technique for enriching your life has been practiced for thousands of years by seekers such as you. Here is what their experience tells us.

If you diligently practice meditation and one-pointedness of mind, you will first of all relinquish the five hindrances and live in a state of joy, happiness and well-being. The second stage will lead you to a deep and tranquil inner calm, with joy and happiness maintained. In the third stage joy disappears and the happiness remains, along with a state of mindful equanimity. The fourth stage will deliver you to a wakeful state of equanimity in which all other sensations disappear. Here you will be completely and totally awake, aware and alive.

But in the meantime, if you practice right effort, right mindfulness and right concentration, you will live in your life moment to moment and surely know that you are doing all you can do. And then just be grateful.

*People are born soft and supple;*
*dead, they are hard and stiff.*
*Plants and trees are born soft and pliant;*
*dead, they are withered and dry.*

*The hard and inflexible*
*are disciples of death.*
*Thus, the soft and yielding*
*are disciples of life.*

*There are no winners among the rigid.*
*If a tree won't bend it will snap in two.*

*Therefore, the rigid and unyielding will be vanquished.*
*The soft and flexible will prevail.*

TAO TE CHING (#76)

*The Sixth Step*

# AS THINGS ARE

■

Gradually, as you work these steps into your life, your view of the world begins to change. Your intuitive understanding of the way things are deepens, and your resolve to continue along this path solidifies. And since these three points are the meat of step six, when you get here it is almost as if this step does itself—especially if you've been diligent about practicing the first five steps. It isn't as though you can coast at this point, but the work you've done so far makes this sixth step feel like a breeze—one that naturally, spontaneously and organically evolved. You may find yourself knowing even before you know. Nothing about this step will seem strange and awkward if you've done the work prior to it. There is still more to be done, of course, and more insight to be gained. But chances are that the strain and resistance you struggled with early on have diminished, the grip that your ego had on you has relaxed and you trust yourself more than ever.

In step two you learned about desire and how it is responsible for so much of your unhappiness and dissatisfaction. You also learned that understanding the causes of your suffering helps you to transcend the craving, which in turn relieves the pain. Here in step six this inner wisdom is further advanced as you awaken to your ultimate truth. In a nonconceptual and nonintellectual way, step six fosters an intuitive understanding that then works its magic as you continue to confront the challenges put before you, especially those concerning work. Here you will finally understand that work is no different from life and life no different from work. You will begin to see the interconnected nature of all things, good and bad. Your dualistic outlook will fall away and a deep sense of wholeness and oneness will take its place. No longer will you be caught in the web of battling egos. Love and compassion will replace anger and hatred, even at work. And you won't think it odd. You will know without a doubt that love and compassion do belong in the workplace (and at home and in the political arena and everyplace else).

*If you wish to shrink something,*
*you must first stretch it.*
*If you wish to weaken something,*
*you must first strengthen it.*
*If you wish to let something go,*
*you must first embrace it.*
*If you wish to have something,*
*you must first give it up.*

*This is called subtle insight*
*into the way things are.*

*The soft overcomes the hard.*
*The weak overcomes the strong.*
*Keep your way a mystery.*
*Let the results speak for themselves.*
      TAO TE CHING (#36)

## Check Your Motives

When you walk out of the house each morning to go to work (or search for a job), what is your intention? Do you intend to have a miserable day, continue yesterday's argument with your coworker or stir up your hatred of the boss and have it color your mood? Or do you make a decision each morning that the day will be a good one, that you will do your best and that others will do their best? Which of the above scenarios promises the better day? The second, of course. And all it takes to get there is a mental shift, a decision, the forming of an intention to enjoy the day. Until you are practiced in doing this, in creating the intention to have a perfect day, you might have to restate your purpose throughout the day, start your day over each time it falls off track and use the tools of the other steps (discipline, concentration, breathing and so on) to help you stay on course.

But as we all know, no matter how clear and strong our intentions, we are constantly presented with challenges that threaten our composure, our resolve. Some of these hindrances are ones we've confronted before, and many of them fall into the main five:

1. Craving (attachment, desire, lust)
2. Ill will (anger, hatred, animosity, resentment)
3. Laziness (languor, torpor, sloth)
4. Restlessness (worry, especially about what happens next)
5. Doubt (skepticism)

So let's begin the lesson of this step by first address-ing these hindrances. And rather than seeing them as barriers or blockades that keep us stalled until we figure out a way around them, let's view them as opportunities. This will give you the chance to practice turning your point of view around and seeing things from the oppo-site direction, which will give you a broader perspective and open your mind to new possibilities.

Generally, anytime you find yourself in the middle of worry or doubt, chances are the central focus is *me*: "What will happen to me?" "They'll never pay attention to me." Whenever you suffer from anger, laziness or craving, the predominant pronoun is again *I* or *me*: "I can't stand that way of doing things." "I'll get to it soon." "I must have that promotion no matter what the cost; it'll make me feel better about myself." But you are not alone in this first-person whirlpool. Most of us are so self-absorbed that whenever anything happens, all we can think about is "How does this affect me?" Because of this self-centeredness we constantly sacrifice opportunities to get in touch with the real truth. We swim in the soup of *me* and learn nothing.

So, with this in mind, let's examine the five challenges and learn how to gain some insight by looking away from *me* and checking our motives.

1. *Ill will, anger, resentment, hatred.* Each time this feeling comes up at work, decide that there is something about the particular situation that you don't know and make the effort to find out what it is. Usually feelings of ill will stem from ignorance and especially ignorance of how the other person feels. Put yourself in his or her position. Try to imagine what the situation feels like to the person. Detach yourself from your own feelings and become an objective observer. Take yourself out of the *me* soup. Acknowledge your hurt but also be aware of the other party's. Engage your empathy. If the anger persists, look at your attachment to it and try to understand why you might be unwilling to let it go. Check your motives.

2. *Craving, desire, lust.* When you want something that isn't there and this desire causes you pain, what is it that you're not seeing? Focused as you are on what isn't, on what you want that you don't have, it's hard to see what is, what you have. So whenever the yearning for something else or more takes you away, refocus your attention on

what you do have. Try to understand why you have the need to pull yourself away into an illusory world. Take five minutes and write a gratitude list. Express gratitude for what you have and see your insatiable desire as an expression of your ego and the result of being stuck in the *me* soup. And again, check your motives.

3. *Laziness, torpor, languor, sloth.* This would include procrastination, a five-syllable word for sloth. How many of us haven't practiced this? But before you go beating yourself up, detach yourself from the tendency to self-flagellate; become the witness to your own life. After all, self-pity is also *me*-directed. Look for the truth instead. Do you procrastinate on certain projects because you dislike doing them, because you imagine they will be hard or boring or because you want everyone to think you have too much to do? The best solution here is to just do it. Don't waste time. Each time you notice yourself slacking off, ask what your intention is. Clarity of mind will foster purpose in action.

4. *Worry, restlessness.* Now that you know the present is all you have and that no one can know the future, you can eliminate worry by just being present. No need to spend time thinking about that promotion or raise. You will know when you know. Worrying about losing your job may actually contribute to your losing it since it will make you inattentive and unproductive. Know-

ing this will help you to detach from useless worry and restless emotions and focus your attention on what actually is happening, not on what might happen.

5. *Doubt.* This often goes hand in hand with any spiritual quest, which is what your work journey is. You may doubt you're in the right job, on the right path, doing the right thing. Don't ignore the questions. Allow them to come up. Face them and find the answers. And be attentive because sometimes fear masquerades as doubt, worry or even anger. If you look closely and penetrate into the truth, you will know, doubt will slip away. Commitment to your life as it is will be deep and rewarding.

Even though you've come this far in the process you won't necessarily be rid of all your problems. You may continue to experience doubt or worry about your future. And you may now and then spend more time than is healthy in *me* indulgence. But you've learned that all of these challenges can teach you something. Every thing, every person, every experience is an opportunity for growth, a teaching of some kind. And gratitude for all of it, the good and the bad, the pleasurable and hurtful, is a must if you are to be free and happy. By simply saying thank you to whatever comes your way, especially the bad, even if you don't mean it yet, you establish right intention.

In this part of the sixth step you begin to notice that if your motive is pure, the results will be unmuddied.

Your intention to do good, to be good, generous or caring, will carry you through and make the difference. If your aim is to hurt someone, then you will. But you will also hurt yourself. So why not turn it around? Set up right intention and the right thing will happen—even if you don't agree with the universe's definition of right. That is not your job. Your job is to do what you can do and keep your resolve and motives truthful. The payoff is gaining a deep and true wisdom that comes only with time, hard work, patience and love.

## The Spirit of Cooperation

When we sit in a selfish, deluded state of mind—the *me* soup—our attitudes turn to poison and taint everything. We see the world through the *me* prism and stand ignorant of what is truly going on. Then our desires and attachment to the way we want things take us over and control us. Next, when the world doesn't conform to our fantasies, we move into a state of aggression and hatred.

This is a pattern that gets repeated over and over again in big and small ways, even during the course of one day, never mind a lifetime. But you can alter this pattern and change your habitual ways of operating simply by directing your attention away from thoughts of "What about me?" to thoughts of "What can I do for you?" In a nutshell, it is imperative that you throw into the mix of your life a large dose of love and compassion. Otherwise you will get lost in the vortex of greed, anger and delusion. Love and compassion are the antidotes to ignorance, aversion and attachment. Love and compassion belong as much at work as they do at home, if only to counteract the meanness that is too often prevalent in the workplace. And this you can do. You can help change the atmosphere at work. You can stop thinking solely about you and begin to think about others. This will bring you more joy and happiness than any other approach—though this should not be your sole motivation, because having such an expectation will only set in motion the cycle of greed, anger and delusion. So be careful here. Do it, but as you do it be loving and compassionate—for its own sake, then for the sake of others and, lastly, for your own sake. Here's why, according to the Dalai Lama: "If you contribute to other people's happiness, you will find the true goal, the true meaning of life." Isn't this what you really want? Isn't this why you've read this far? Isn't it in fact what we all want? To the Dalai Lama's sentiment we can add, *When you behave in a loving and compassionate way while at work, your day-to-day satisfaction on the job will increase.*

Try it. You will experience a pleasant shift in no time at all. Here are some suggested ways of expressing this attitude at work and of using it to counteract the *me* syndrome.

1. Sometimes you may think your focus is on others, as you watch them get a promotion or accolades from the boss or some other perk related to the job. But too often, even as you congratulate them,

you may harbor feelings of resentment and self-pity. Next time put your anger aside and imagine yourself in your coworkers' shoes. Feel their joy. Be happy for them. Don't look at what you don't have. Take the focus off you—let it be on them, with love in your heart. If you can't yet feel the love, be at least willing to be happy for them. Create that intention in your heart.

2. If one of your colleagues falls behind in his or her work, lend a helping hand. And before you lapse into judgment, and without acting superior, attempt to discover why the person is behind—become a compassionate listener if your coworker is willing to open up (without jeopardizing either job, and keeping the focus on work). Maybe he has a personal problem or injury that's interfering with his productivity and only needs help in the short term but was too proud to ask. Or maybe she's new on the job and needs more training. If the person has nothing to say, simply offer your assistance with an open heart. Help out where you can without becoming a martyr or enabling someone else. Realize that when every member of the team is efficient, everyone wins.

3. Learn to be a team player. Don't just look out for number one. Become a worker among workers, no head higher than any other. Don't play the big shot. And if someone else does, don't engage in battle. Think about and do what's best for the group. Keep your ego out of it but do your best.

If there's a troublemaker in the group, express kindness toward this person. Notice the effect. Be awake and aware at all times. Be involved in the process and not in your own small mind. Park your petty ego outside the door and work with your healthy one—the one that thinks and behaves in estimable ways and can take care of you without taking the events of the day personally, the one that can rise above any mean-spiritedness and not boast about it.

4. If your motivation in practicing loving-kindness at work is to make people like you, cease and desist at once. It is not in your control, and in the end it is none of your business who likes you. What is your business is loving and caring for all those around you, even if you don't like some of them so much. Treat everyone with the love and respect that you yourself deserve and at the end of the day you will be at peace with yourself.

5. Be generous with your ideas, your knowledge and your expertise, without being foolhardy. Share what you know. Don't keep secrets. If someone walks away with one of your ideas and claims credit for it, have compassion for him and believe that he needed it more than you. Express gratitude for having this person in your life and trust that you will someday know why he is there. Don't be stingy with yourself. Your gifts are just that, gifts, to be shared with the world. Nothing withers the spirit more than repression and stinginess.

6. This suggestion was offered earlier and bears repeating: engage on a regular basis in anonymous acts of charity. Do something nice for someone at work and tell no one. Do this especially for someone who has hurt you or for whom you hold bad feelings. And don't make it so obvious that the benefactor can be none other than you. Anonymity here is most important. Notice the impact that such an act has on the receiver, if you are in a position to notice. Best of all is simply doing, walking away and letting go. Just be awake to its effect on you.

You might ask, as Chris did, what you can do when a boss (or coworker) is mean, hungry for power and constantly critical. Chris's current situation at work is typical, as is his new boss, Lori. You may be tempted here to assign gender as the cause of their problem, but don't be so quick to judge. A dynamic like that between Chris and Lori can arise anywhere with anyone. Use this story as an opportunity to look closely at both sides before deciding who is right, who is wrong and what the appropriate course of action would be.

Chris has been with his company for twenty years. He has been manager of his department for ten, makes a decent living, rather likes what he does and takes pride in his work. He has no ambition to move up to higher management, gets along well enough with his bosses, but keeps his distance from them as much as possible. Chris, dependable and hardworking, spends all of his free time with his cherished family. Recently Chris was transferred to a new store location—his experience and expertise were needed to help the store and his department in particular recover from the effects of a poor manager. Chris wasn't thrilled with the move—it meant working longer and harder for a while—but he didn't complain and was up for the challenge. His managers left him pretty much on his own, and they were not disappointed.

A few months after this move Lori was brought in to be his immediate supervisor. Almost at once Lori started throwing her authority around, and according to Chris and the rest of the staff, she didn't do it very nicely. In fact, she was mean and judgmental and tended to personalize her criticism. The morale in the store sank as she began initiating changes that affected the way the other employees performed their jobs. She insisted that everyone work faster, she was quick to write anyone up for the least little infraction without even considering the consequences, and she forced everyone to take a full hour for their meal break rather than the usual half hour—all of this just for starters. Chris didn't want an hour lunch since it meant less time with his family. And even though he would be off the clock during the hour, he knew (and most likely Lori knew) that he'd work during much of this time anyway, since the work is never really done and he has a sense of proprietorship about his department.

All of this led Chris to dislike his new boss, to resist the changes that she was making and to lapse into a state where he actually dreaded going to work. Chris was not alone in his reactions. Many other associates responded similarly. They complained to each other, wondered what was to be done and blamed upper management for their predicament. How could these managers be so uncaring and disregarding of the employees' welfare as to give them Lori as a boss, after all the sweat and years they had given the company?

It is so easy here to take sides, blame Lori and rail at the injustice of it all. But let's look at the situation from a different angle, since we know that this reflexive stance will only create anger and dissatisfaction, which will trigger a downward spiral that will not only affect job performance but poison the work atmosphere and contribute to the destruction of morale and the rise of despair.

And let's keep the analysis simple and not get into personalities—always a good course to follow.

1. Chris has been at his job a long time, cares about his work and has become accustomed to working on his own without management interference.
2. Lori is clearly a hands-on manager, even if her tactics are alienating. And she has some agenda whose source might even be her own boss.
3. Everyone is frustrated with Lori's style and her attempts to assert her authority. She means to let everyone know that she's the boss.
4. Lori is the boss. For better or worse.

5. The sooner Chris accepts and stops resisting the fact that Lori is the boss the easier his job will be.
6. Change is difficult, especially when the agent of that change is unpleasant.
7. Resistance to change is normal but not necessary. The less resistance, the smoother the course and the quicker the acceptance.
8. There is a tug-of-war between Lori's and Chris's egos: "My way of doing things is best." "You're wrong, mine is the better way."
9. The first one to give up this struggle will be the winner.

So what can Chris do to reestablish his balance and foster harmony? (We could offer suggestions for Lori as well, but since in reality we can only change our side of things, let's just examine the effect of one-sided change.) Chris can first accept that Lori is his boss and that even if he disagrees with her management style, he must abide by the new rules. (If there were moral or ethical issues at stake, the tack would be different.) Chris can then do as he is told and let go of *his* need to be right and *his* desire to do things in a certain way. He can then behave in a loving and compassionate way toward Lori. Without irony or self-righteousness Chris can let Lori know that he recognizes her authority. He can put himself in her shoes and try to understand how difficult it must be to come into a new place and establish authority with people who have been entrenched in their jobs for a very long time. Chris can do his work as Lori dictates. Time will tell which is the better way. At this moment it is not Chris's business to know. In the meantime there will be peace at work, and Chris can return to some semblance of calm and to enjoying his work again. His resentment toward Lori may not disappear at once and may even grow deeper as he reluctantly follows Lori's directions. Chris can then pray that Lori gets everything she wants, that she is happy and at peace. Every time Chris's anger toward Lori surfaces, he can wish the best for her rather than indulge the anger. There is no better weapon against meanness than kindness. Chris can do Lori's bidding with a smile on his face. And without becoming a sycophant, Chris can do more than Lori asks and do it with good humor. The tendency in this type of situation is to withhold and do the very least that is required. Chris can notice his inclination toward this and do the opposite. Chris's new attitude and behavior may have no effect whatsoever on Lori and her style. And it really doesn't matter. The intention here is not to change Lori. What Chris's new outlook will affect, and very powerfully, is Chris himself. By opening his heart to love and compassion rather than clenching it in anger and fear, he will be happier. And his mood will have an effect on others. (Ever notice how someone's bad mood can infect the whole office? Keep in mind that it works the other way too.) And as we've said before, work is not different and separate from life, so Chris's home life will also benefit, since as hard as he could try to leave his negative feelings toward Lori at work, he wouldn't be very successful. And as hard as it will be for him to muster up love and compassion toward Lori when he's not getting what he wants, it's a heck of a lot easier, and a whole lot more pleasant, than living with dislike and disharmony.

And Chris can view the hour lunch break as a gift rather than a burden. For some time Chris has been complaining (despite his love for his family) about having no time for himself. Taking the full hour given to him—for himself—and not working (after all, the job is never done anyway, and the boss has demanded he take the full hour) will give him an opportunity to be alone, to practice some of the suggestions here and to return to his job and family refreshed and reinvigorated. If he insists on living in resentment and hostility, his job, his family and he will suffer for it. But if he can bring himself around to enjoying this gift of time, then everyone can benefit. Who knows, he may even end up being grateful to Lori. And as he begins to treat himself better he may also begin to treat her better. As they say in the business world, this is a win-win situation.

## When You're the Boss

We live in a world of paradox, yet too often we do not see how we are responsible. By taking responsibility for our own life, our own actions, our own work, we can reduce the frustration and disappointment created by our perpetual yearning for something other than what we have. And no matter what your job is or whom you work for, it is imperative that you view yourself as your own boss. Stop waiting for the external circumstances to change in your favor or for the other party (your boss or partner) to come to his or her senses and do the right thing. In the end your happiness is in your hands. And even before the end, right now, it is up to you.

When we are unhappy at work we attempt to reach an understanding of why we're so unhappy, and we usually look around us to see what's up, to get a fix on what's causing the pain. We often see work as the problem and convince ourselves that it needs fixing. We fail to notice that it is our relationship to work that we are having trouble with, not the work itself. The relationship we develop with work is not so unlike the bonds we form or want to form with the people in our lives. We can learn a lot about our connection to work by looking at our other relationships, and vice versa. We may think that they're different because work is not a thinking, breathing entity. But they're not so different. First of all, work is not static, but what's most important to look at here is how we relate to work, not how it relates to us—and this is the pivotal point that will bring understanding to all our relationships. If we can penetrate and understand the workings of this, then all confusion and dissatisfaction will disappear. So in order to understand the dynamics of the work relationship a little better, let's take a moment to examine a relationship that cannot be defined any other way—an intimate one. And even if you are not currently in one, each of you has had some experience with a close relationship, be it with a parent, friend, lover, child or neighbor—someone else you wanted or needed to get along with.

Usually when we are involved in a close relationship we have needs and expectations that we want satisfied. And whether we realize it or not, by depending on the other person for our inner contentment, we give them power over us. Even when we don't clearly communicate our needs we expect the other person to know what they are, especially if they purport to love us. And when we do communicate what we want from them we are crushed even more when they don't comply. We again state our needs. They again fail us. We don't understand how they can be so cruel. Maybe we leave them, maybe we keep trying. This scenario continues with the same or different partners. We try different things in order to be understood. It's as if we're stuck in some rut, and the harder we try, the more entrenched we get. We do the same thing over and over and each time expect different results, even though history tells us not to. Or we move through a series of intimate relationships thinking that the next one will be it, the next one will conform to our ideal. There is a perfect someone out there; all we need to do is find this person. Any of this sound familiar?

What we don't see when we are in this rut is that our understanding of the problem itself is limited. We see the problem only in terms of the other person's behavior. Even if we change ours and only concentrate on our side, we still harbor expectations or hope that they will change too. We settle in—even when we're not getting our needs met and are basically unhappy—and gain some comfort from the familiarity of our situation. Then we tell ourselves it won't always be this way (our innate wisdom knows that nothing is permanent) and hope for the best (a form of delusion and denial) but fail to do anything about it, or move on to the next someone and end up creating a yet deeper rut (our conditioned existence).

And when it comes to work, our conditioned behavior is carried with us. So if we're unhappy, either we resign ourselves to our misery, knowing that the work won't or can't change, or we keep moving on, searching for the perfect job. But this is no different from how we handle our other relationships—we still look at the work as the problem. If we're honest with ourselves and closely observe the historical evidence, we know that the solution to our dissatisfaction lies elsewhere. It is time to understand rather than keep trying to be understood. We need to understand the truth, the reality of our condition, before we can know what to do. The surface knowledge is easy and usually where we stop. What isn't so easy is gaining a deeper understanding. For this we need a clear mind and an open heart. We need to view the people in our lives and ourselves without judgment, expectation, jealousy or selfishness. We need to see the other person as he or she is. We need to see our work as it is, not as we would like it to be, not as we think it should be. We need to see that no one can do for us what we cannot do for ourselves. We need to see how our desire for this other person (or our company, boss, coworker, job) to conform to what we think is right, appropriate and good only obfuscates our vision. When we pull ourselves out of the rut, even for a short while, we have a chance to learn what the truth really is. This is how we are our own boss.

And so our relationship with work—no matter the circumstances—can be one in which we are in charge, where we accept what is and understand that no one else is responsible for our day-to-day satisfaction. Once we embrace this, we empower ourselves to make changes if necessary, to move forward when ready and to truly know that loving what we do is our choice and that we can make that choice at any moment.

## Wise Men Can Dance

In this part of the sixth step we complete the circle and establish the connection with the other five steps. What completes it is wisdom. Wisdom combines an intellectual knowledge about the way things are with a deeper intuitive sense of the true nature of things, leading to a perfect understanding of the workings of the universe. Here we understand that this process is a circular rather than a linear one. You can begin the whole process right here in this step, right now. All you need to do is to see things as they are. Not as they once were or as they might be or as you want them to be, but as they are. No good or bad about it. Just the way things are. No judgment. No labeling. Just what *is*.

Here in this step, especially if you've already done the others, you have a perfect view of things as they are. And once here, once you understand fully and deeply, in an intuitive rather than intellectual way, how things are, then there is no struggle with the need to be happy. You are, without dwelling on it, content with your life, with the way things are, even as you continue to grow and deepen your insight.

Here is what you've learned so far:

1. The truth of impermanence—things change.
2. Your attachments and the desire for things to be different from how they are cause you to suffer.
3. When you stay out of the past and the future and bring yourself into each present moment, it is possible to be happy.
4. What you do and say, and how you do it and say it, determines how harmoniously balanced your life will be.
5. By making an effort and practicing mindfulness and concentration, you can achieve deep satisfaction in all that you do.
6. By opening your heart and expressing compassion for all things, you have an opportunity to gain deep insight into the way of all things and acceptance of the way things are.

One poignant way to be filled with life, to be happy each moment and to be more carefree, is to accept that one day you will die. Before you recoil from this subject, pick up some of the tools that you've learned in order to stay on course. And rather than view the topic of death as morbid, see it as just another aspect of life, one that will affirm and enrich it.

If you accept that nothing in life is permanent, then you're aware that this includes your life as you know it. No big deal. Just what is. In fact, as each new moment passes, your life is different. If you have had a small inkling of how your attachments to life and the things in it can cause you pain, then maybe you are ready to consider that by accepting the fact that you will die, thus letting go of your attachment to life, your life will be ecstatic. And when death comes you will be ready.

We hear all the time about people who have had brushes with death or who have contracted life-threatening illnesses and have gone on to live fuller and richer lives as a result. Each moment becomes important, a gift not to be wasted. With the fear of death removed, an intense love of life takes its place. When we hold on to anything too tightly life is drained from it. So facing our own assured death will loosen our grip on life and allow us to embrace it with love rather than fear.

So stop waiting for your life to happen, for the right job to surface. Life is happening now. Don't wait for your life to be threatened before you acknowledge that it won't last forever. Face your death now so that you might live now.

And as far as your work is concerned, don't view it as a rigid, static object that you must accept and maneuver your way around so as not to get hurt. Instead, gently take hold of your work as you would a dance partner (even if it is a large and clumsy one) and teach it the steps you know, accepting its moves and limitations. Take turns leading. Take pleasure in the music, in the flow of the choreography. Allow both grace and awkwardness into the mix on both sides. There is something to learn from all partners. If you are patient and alert, you will know if and when you need to change partners. With practice you will become flexible, proficient and compassionate. And you will be in the middle of the ballroom of your life, as you are now, as it cannot be otherwise. You will know exactly where you are, you will be at peace with this knowledge and the joy that fills your heart will know no bounds.

As-it-is is as it should be.

*Look, and it can't be seen.*
*Listen, and it can't be heard.*
*Reach, and it can't be grasped.*

*Formless, soundless, subtle.*
*All three return into nothing*
*and merge together as one.*
*One—it stands uniquely on its own*
*and yet encompasses all things.*

*Unnamable, boundless,*
*it returns to the state of nothing.*
*The form that has no form.*
*The image that has no substance.*
*This is beyond imagining.*

*Follow it and you see no end.*
*Confront it and you see no beginning.*
*All you can do is be in the present.*
*Know where you came from*
*but live in today.*
*This is the way to serenity.*

TAO TE CHING (#14)

## The Seventh Step
# YOU'RE ALREADY
# THERE

■

The seventh step is the easiest and at the same time the most difficult. It is the one that you work without even thinking about it as you make your way through the first six steps. It is the one that you live in when your mind is at rest and your heart open. It is the one that reminds you to tap into your child spirit and not take the world and yourself so seriously. It is:

*JUST BE*

And right here is where this step could end. But because my publisher and you the reader most likely have expectations that if indeed this is a step in the process, there should be more, I will elaborate. If you wanted to, though, you could stop reading right now and get the full impact of the message of this book:

*JUST BE*

There are three essential points in the first six steps that carry you to this seventh one and help you to *just be*.

1. *Impermanence.* Since everything changes and you cannot predict how, your only choice here, and the one that will lead you to peace of mind, is:

*EXPECT NOTHING*

2. *Suffering.* Your pervasive dissatisfaction with the way things are is caused by your desires, delusions and attachments. There is one exercise that you can perform every day that will ease your suffering. Each day in stillness and with deep concentration you can

*JUST SIT*

3. *Nonself.* When you sit in your *me* soup you have to ask yourself, "Who is this *me* that I'm so steeped in?" If you then realize that this self consists of your six faculties and five conditioned states, you can let go of the idea that there is a self operating behind all this, and then you can extract yourself from the *me* soup. This then will free you from the tyranny of your ego and allow you to

*BE GRATEFUL*

So by just sitting, with no expectations, we can adopt gratitude, and no matter what happens we will not judge. No matter how things turn out we will see the benefits. We will not try to control the events of our lives or the people in them, yet we will participate fully and joyfully. We will just be. We will say thank you even for the bad because it is not up to us to define or determine what is bad. And when we do, when we have distance and perspective on this bad thing, we will see how it was in fact good. We will *just be* in each moment, mindfully attentive and awake. And this awakened state of mind will then lead us to

*IMPERTURBABILITY*
*EQUANIMITY*
*COMPASSION*

With these newly acquired attitudes, we can love whatever it is we're doing. We can treat others with respect and care. We can feel grateful at the close of each day for exactly everything. It's impossible to have it any other way as long as we are *just being.*

And then once again we can return to the three principles that were introduced in the very beginning. We can use them as guiding lights, pointing the way and encouraging us.

*SIMPLICITY*
*PATIENCE*
*COMPASSION*

As all these new ideas and fresh approaches swim in your head, allow yourself to relax, to just be and to trust that if you rely on yourself, your path will be clear. You will know what to do and when to do it. Your work will become a joy as you incorporate these seven steps into your life. You will see that you already know what your work is meant to be. You will understand what it is that you must do to make your way toward it, if you're not already in it. And in the process you will appreciate each small step. There will no longer be the thought that when you finally get to do what you want to do, then you will be happy. Instead you will be happy doing what you're doing. Now. This moment will hold all there is, and you will know it. All that is left for you to do is

*JUST BE*

And then

*EXPECT NOTHING*
*JUST SIT*
*EXPRESS GRATITUDE*

That's it. And when you take a moment to be in the silence, in the stillness of this moment, you will know that you are already there.

*Still your body.*
*Quiet your mind.*
*Watch as all things rise up*
*and then observe their return.*
*All beings arise from the same source*
*and each one returns to its roots.*
*This is called tranquility.*

*To find serenity return to the source.*
*Grounded in serenity you gain insight.*
*Without this you will be confused and unhappy.*
*With it you will become*
*tolerant and impartial,*
*compassionate and wise,*
*patient and contented.*

*Embracing the way of all things*
*you accept what life brings,*
*and when death comes, you are ready.*

TAO TE CHING (#16)

# BIBLIOGRAPHY

∎

The selections from the *Tao Te Ching* are all new renderings by the author. The following texts were used:

Henricks, Robert G., trans., *Te-Tao Ching*, by Lao-Tzu. New York: Ballantine Books, 1989.

Lau, D. C., trans., *Tao Te Ching*, by Lao Tzu. London: Penguin Books, 1963.

Mair, Victor H., trans., *Tao Te Ching*, by Lao Tzu. New York: Bantam Books, 1990.

Mitchell, Stephen, trans., *Tao Te Ching*, by Lao Tzu. New York: Harper and Row, 1988.

Wu, John C. H., trans., *Tao Teh Ching*, by Lao Tzu. Boston: Shambhala Publications, 1961.

*About the Author*

Nancy O'Hara was drawn to Zen Buddhism in the mid-1980s after her father died and found solace there in the profound stillness of silent meditation. After living in a Zen monastery in the early nineties, Nancy became even more dedicated to her practice and passionate about sharing with others the mindful approach to living that her teacher, Eido Shimano Roshi, and the other monks had taught her. Since before her first book, *Find a Quiet Corner*, was published in 1995, she has been conducting workshops and retreats for seekers interested in Buddhist teachings through a Western-mind filter.

Nancy spent more than twenty years in the corporate arena working for both large and small firms and left that world in the mid-1990s to venture out on her own. Those years spent inside corporate America have given Nancy a keen insight into the challenges we all face every day on the job and the importance of balancing mind and body, soul and spirit. With one foot firmly planted in the West and the other in the East, Nancy O'Hara brings to us a rich and powerful message laced with simplicity and compassion.

Currently a full-time author and teacher, Nancy shares her unique approach to a peaceful life in workshops, retreats, and corporate seminars. Nancy continues to live in New York City, rather than on the top of a mountain waiting for enlightenment, because she believes the truth is to be found in the daily rituals of our ordinary lives.